TAKE THIS

Get Instant Access to Your **FREE**
Expert Assessment...

"The Generational Personality Test"
(a $15 value)

**DISCOVER WHAT GENERATION YOU REALLY
BELONG TO AND WHAT THAT MEANS FOR YOUR WORK
WITH MILLENNIALS**

AGE HAS NOTHING TO DO WITH IT!
Take the Quiz Now at...

WWW.QUIZ.MILLENNIALSOLUTION.COM

FREE QUIZ NOW!

ADVANCED PRAISE FOR
5 MILLENNIAL MYTHS

With one foot firmly planted in the Millennials' world and her other in the business world, Gabrielle Bosché understands clearly the problems of supervising Millennials in the workplace. She identifies five commonly held myths and systematically analyzes, and debunks, each one. More important, Gabrielle gives specific, practical, step-by-step advice on ways for supervisors to motivate and mentor Millennials for maximum productivity and success.

Morton Blackwell
      President of The Leadership Institute

5 Millennial Myths is a fast paced, spot on, eminently practical guide for both Millennials and those who would employ, partner, and collaborate with them. Gabrielle writes with clarity and conviction. Our Senior Leadership team will be reading this guide!

Dr. John Jackson
      President of William Jessup University and the author of
      six books on Leadership, Communication, and Spiritual
      Growth

5 Millennial Myths: The Handbook for Motivating and Managing Millennials is a fantastic read and resource. As a member of an organization that continually strives for effective and appropriate communication, I can appreciate a body of work that successfully outlines strategies to bridge the communication gap between generations. I found this to be incredibly resourceful. I would recommend this book to managers, educators and even to Millennials.

Jacqueline Northrop
Principal Consultant and Founder of Scarlet Communications

Gabrielle Bosché has done a marvelous job at dispelling the five common myths about working with Millennials in the workplace, and, in doing so, provides us with clear and thorough descriptions of who Millennials are and how they think. If you are a manager or leader in the workplace and have Millennials working with and for you, this is a must read since we must adapt to the new generation if we are to see them use their energy and creativity to help our organizations.

Bruce E. Winston, PhD
Professor of Business and Leadership
Regent University
Virginia Beach, Virginia USA

Gabrielle Bosché gives us an honest portrayal of her generation and how we can best leverage their amazing strengths. This little handbook, along with giving great advice to Millennials, is a must have for managers and leaders.

Jeremy Dunlap
Business speaker and author of *Danny: The Virtues Within (What America Can Learn from Navy SEAL Danny Dietz)*

ALSO BY ...

GABRIELLE BOSCHÉ

THE MILLENNIAL SOLUTION: TAPPING THE NEXT
  GENERATION OF TALENT
THE MILLENNIAL ENTREPRENEUR: SIDE-HUSTLERS,
  STARTUPS AND DISRUPTERS RESTARTING AMERICA

OTHER RESOURCES BY ...

THE MILLENNIAL SOLUTION

THE MILLENNIAL MANAGEMENT INSTITUTE

THE GUIDE TO HIRING AND INTERVIEWING MILLENNIALS

THE MILLENNIAL ENGAGEMENT CASE STUDY
  (IN PARTNERSHIP WITH THE CATHOLIC
  UNIVERSITY OF AMERICA)

Available exclusively at www.MillennialSolution.com

5 MILLENNIAL MYTHS

THE HANDBOOK FOR MANAGING AND MOTIVATING MILLENNIALS

GABRIELLE BOSCHÉ

SECOND EDITION

Published by BeReadyMEDIA, LLC.
Printed in the United States of America.

To my Creator...

The true reconciler of generations.

To my Husband...

*My fellow dreamer, life partner and love of my life.
You inspire me every day.*

To my Family...

*My roots, constant supports and
encouragers every dreamer needs.*

To You...

*The leaders and mentors who will partner with a new
generation.*

TABLE OF VALUES & FREE DOWNLOADS

PREFACE

INTRODUCTION: THE PROBLEM YOU KNEW YOU HAD

1. MYTH 1: ENTITLED
   "MILLENNIALS THINK THEY DESERVE EVERYTHING"
   - HOW MILLENNIALS GOT TO BE SO ENTITLED
   - TAPPING INTO THEIR AMBITION TODAY
   - MISTAKES EVERY LEADER MAKES BY NOT UNDERSTANDING HOW MILLENNIALS WERE RAISED

2. MYTH 2: DISLOYAL
   "MILLENNIALS ONLY CARE ABOUT THEMSELVES"
   - THE REAL REASON MILLENNIALS QUIT
   - WHY PAYING THEM MORE MONEY NEVER WORKS
   - RETENTION STRATEGIES FOR MANAGERS AND MARKETERS

   BONUS! INTERVIEW SECRETS TO HIRE THE BEST YOUNG TALENT

3. MYTH 3: INDEPENDENT
   "MILLENNIALS DON'T WANT TO WORK WITH US"
   - MENTORING STRATEGIES THAT ARE FREE
   - CREATING A CULTURE MILLENNIALS LOVE... AND EVERYONE ELSE DOESN'T HATE

   BONUS! HOW TO MENTOR A MILLENNIAL

4. MYTH 4: ADDICTED TO TECHNOLOGY
   "DO MILLENNIALS EVER STOP TEXTING?"
   - HOW TO GET MILLENNIALS OFF THEIR PHONES
   - COMMUNICATIONS TECHNQIUES YOU NEED NOW
   - WHY SOCIAL MEDIA COULD KILL YOUR WORKFORCE PRODUCTIVITY

   BONUS! SOCIAL MEDIA POLICY TEMPLATE

5. MYTH 5: UNMOTIVATED
   "HOW DO YOU GET MILLENNIALS TO DO ANYTHING?"
   - SCIENCTIFIC STRATEGIES TO MOTIVATE TWENTY-SOMETHINGS
   - TRANSLATING YOUR MISSION INTO "MILLENNIAL"

   BONUS: CASE STUDY ON HOW TO MOTIVATE A MILLENNIAL

8. THE UNSPOKEN MYTH: MILLENNIALS HATE THEIR PARENTS
"MENTORING AND LEADING THE NEXT GENERATION"
- LEADING YOUR ADULT CHILDREN
- HOW TO LAUNCH YOUR MILLENNIAL
- COACHING MILLENNIALS TO RESPECT LEADERSHIP

9. CONCLUSION: GOING FROM "NOW WHAT?" TO NEXT STEPS
- CORPORATE SOLUTIONS YOU NEED NOW
- TEACHING YOUR TEAM
- MEASURING SUCCESS

INTRODUCTION

It has been less than three years since the first edition of *5 Millennial Myths* was published. And if I'm honest, I am still amazed by what an amazing reception this book has had. I have received emails, texts and Facebook messages from people around the world who have read and loved this book. It has become a part of university business curriculum and company book clubs nationwide.

I wrote *5 Millennial Myths* because there was a hole in the market. Too many people were complaining about my generation, and there was no voice to present an honest case for generational reconciliation.

Since launching, *5 Millennial Myths* has grown from a book into an international training and consulting company. It has landed me in front of Fortune 500 companies and before top military generals around the world. It has allowed me to develop Millennial engagement strategies for government agencies, small nonprofits and presidential campaigns.

I decided to publish a second edition to showcase the new research I have collected while interviewing hundreds of Millennials in focus groups and exit interviews and answering the most common questions leaders, executive and parents raise.

Nearly every single time I get off the stage at a conference, a member of the audience approaches me and explains in their own way, "You helped me understand my kids so much better!" I was asked multiple times to write a book on parenting Millennials. I declined each time because I was in the middle of writing my third book, *The Millennial Entrepreneur: Side-hustlers, Startups and Disrupters Restarting America.* Instead, I developed a massive chapter on how parents of Millennials can mentor, lead and work with their Millennial kids—from teens to adults.

Much of the core content in this book stands but is enhanced with a fresh and more defined list of strategies for leaders to use. I'm not sure about you, but I get frustrated with business books that promise results but are just one long narrative. You don't have time for long-winded answers. You need results! I spent serious time with my editors making sure we got to the good stuff faster and more frequently.

In the spirit of getting down to business, I have included four new downloads throughout the book as a free resource to you. They include relevant case studies we have conducted, internal assessments used by top companies and hiring and interviewing guides. These are just a fraction of the free resources, including webinars, relevant white papers, and audiobooks, you can find at www.millennialsolution.com.

If this is your first introduction to *5 Millennial Myths*, welcome. If you are a loyal part of our community at The Millennial Solution, I want to thank you and welcome you back. Your feedback, partnership and passion fuel our work every day.

BACK TO THE INTRODUCTION

Sitting in his office with the door closed, Phil has just finished reading the email. The company's sales are down and leadership is considering closing his branch. Their overhead is too high, and the team he leads hasn't closed two consecutive sales quarters in the black in over two years.

Phil looks up to see Kayla, his 24-year-old sales representative, standing at the door signaling to see if she can come in. Though she is meeting with him to discuss her upcoming vacation schedule, Phil's mind is still on the email, so he asks,

"Do you think we could cut our operating cost by 25 percent and still keep our clients happy?"

She pauses for a moment, then says,

"When I was in college, each dorm had a challenge to reduce our water bottle usage by half in one year. The winning dorm got free pizza for a week and these funny T-shirts that said 'I'm not trashy.' Maybe we could make it a competition and ask everyone here to come up with ideas on reducing their own waste?"

Phil puts out the challenge to his team, and three days later, four of his least experienced employees step into his office to make a pitch. Phil is expecting a simple conversation, but they pull out an iPad and begin a presentation that rolls from slide to slide with slick infographics, comparable practices of the competition, and quirky photos of the staff themselves. It isn't just fun to watch; to Phil's surprise, the presenters actually have solid ideas that include the following

- Let employees with kids work from home
- Use an e-check deposit system and go paperless in one year
- Partner with the local university to conduct market research
- Launch a social media marketing campaign
- Host a podcast.

Phil has never considered any of these concepts before. With just a few years of work experience under their belts, these twenty-somethings are thinking more outside of the box than his seasoned staff. Phil decides to go with some of their ideas—even the risky ones—and is shocked when they volunteer to coordinate everything for him.

Ten months later, the company is on track to significantly reduce the amount of paper products in the office. It has streamlined its accounting process after downloading new software. It's also saved thousands of dollars on travel by using video conference calls to meet with prospective clients. Best of all, Phil's employees are more engaged at work and have even taken the initiative to come up with other ideas to better optimize staff time by combining positions.

This makes Phil wonder what other treasures are hidden amongst his staff. From simple fixes to multi-year profit plans, even his greenest employees have personal experience or insight to contribute. Even better, the more he incorporates younger staff, the longer they stay in the company—and even take on responsibilities outside of their assigned roles.

READY OR NOT, HERE WE COME

Millennials are graduating from college and flooding the workforce in record numbers. We are the largest and most educated generation to compete for jobs in American history.

So how do you attract, retain, and manage a generation that looks and acts like your kids?

If you are clueless about what to do with us, you're not alone! Managers everywhere are frustrated with the high turnover, lack of professionalism, low productivity, and increased costs associated with Millennials.

The ability to effectively leverage next-generation talent will be the driving factor for success in the new economy. But as Albert Einstein stated, "In the middle of difficulty lies opportunity."

5 Millennial Myths will give you the tools to turn your next-generation talent into rocket fuel, launching your company's creative success. Learn the techniques that empower and inspire Millennial employees to use their entrepreneurial drive at work. Turn the caricature of today's youth on its head and give your office culture a facelift. Break down generational communication barriers and create an engaging and dynamic work environment that highlights every team member's strengths. Increase your organization's long-term profit by keeping quality talent while discovering the unlocked potential of those you manage.

This book is full of practical tips and plug-and-play applications, all designed from peer-reviewed research, personal experience, and popular media. It is structured in a way that will allow you to quickly understand the top five myths about the next generation, then discover the best practices for harnessing Millennials' hidden strengths and turning them into your company's strengths. Each chapter also includes Tips for both managers and Millennials to achieve immediate application of the information covered in the book.

CUT YOUR LOSSES

Companies are losing out on millions in profit because of high turnover and a management style that is unknowingly stifling the Millennial drive, rather than embracing it. The ones losing the most are those who are hiring positions rather than people. It is these individuals who fail to see how their employees' youth and inexperience is an asset, not a liability.

The average cost of turnover is 50 percent of an employee's salary. That means that if a Millennial employee making $45,000 leaves after one year, that company has instantly lost $22,000[1]. If two of her friends join her in leaving, that's $66,000. For a company of 700 employees experiencing 10 percent annual turnover, it's a loss of $1.5 million. That's not even counting the money left on the table if those employees had the potential to take the organization into greater levels of productivity!

Across industries, managers are failing to see just how simple it is—whether their goal is attracting quality Millennial talent to their firm, growing youth membership in their organization, or increasing enrollment in an educational program.

Managers don't need to throw away money on a slick new media campaign, hire a celebrity spokesperson, or replace all of their office furniture with giant beanbag chairs. They just need to learn who Millennials are and—more importantly—who they are not.

THIS IS A BOOK ABOUT MILLENNIALS BY A MILLENNIAL

There is truth in the myths. Millennials are entitled, disloyal, independent, addicted to technology, and unmotivated. We have a reputation, and we have earned it. We expect a job but don't want to work. We think we deserve the promotion, even though we just started six months ago. We want the recognition without the sacrifice.

Although I understand the frustration of our managers, parents, and professors, I don't see a group of teenagers and twenty-somethings out for themselves and unengaged in the world. When I look at my generation, I see creativity, a view of life that knows no limits, and a love of diversity. This book will help you get into the Millennial mind and see the challenge as an opportunity, transforming the roadblock into a stepping-stone.

We don't want to be managed. We want to be led.

The first step to leading Millennials is to understand what makes us tick—what motivates us, what gets us to work harder, and even what turns us off completely. We can be a secret weapon for those who know how to tap into our creativity, drive, and ambition. We want to be empowered rather than micromanaged, trusted rather than second-guessed, inspired rather than taken advantage of.

That twenty-something who is fixing your car today could be running your company tomorrow. This is a handbook to understanding and successfully integrating the Millennial drive. Don't write us off yet. We're just getting started.

CHAPTER 1
MYTH 1: MILLENNIALS ARE ENTITLED

Walk into Facebook's Silicon Valley headquarters and you will find a simple phrase inscribed on the wall: "Move Fast and Break Things." This isn't just the company's approach to business, but its approach to life.

When Mark Zuckerberg first started out in the tech-start up world, the media called him the "toddler CEO." After all, who did this kid think he was? How did he know what he was doing? Why would a twenty-something think he had what it took to run a multi-million (now billion) dollar company?

Anyone who was a sceptic then is a convert now. Zuckerberg and his team of caffeine-fueled Millennials refused to take "no" for an answer. They saw a gap in the market, decided to take a different approach to business and worked tirelessly to turn their dream into reality. Mark Zuckerberg and his friends didn't build the social networking giant on their own; they relied on investors who believed in the product, advisors who had built successful companies, and staff ambitious enough to think they could pull it off. What looked like entitlement to the world was really just relentless ambition.

This is not unique to the Millennial generation. Any entrepreneur knows that everyone is a critic on the way up, and this is even truer on the way down. Steve Jobs and Bill Gates experienced much of the same criticism and challenges as Zuckerberg did. But unlike the start-up titans of the Xer and Boomer generations, Millennials are coming across as entitled rather than innovative, deserving rather than driven.

HOW MILLENNIALS GOT SO ENTITLED

Each month I take someone out to lunch whose life and career inspires me. It was at one of these meetings when a business owner unknowingly pitched the idea for this book. We soon began talking about the high turnover of young professionals in the area and what it was like trying to keep quality Millennials.

"I don't know what it is," she explained. "But these Millennials just don't want to stick around. And when they do, they expect to be promoted in the first six months!"

I nodded in complete agreement, although I was secretly guilty of the same sentiment. If employees don't see any prospect of promotion, why shouldn't they advance their careers in other ways? Sure, six months is a short amount of time, but for a 23-year-old, it is two percent of his or her current life-span.

Setting personal bias aside though, I understood this business owner's point. Today's young professionals appear to believe crossing the graduation platform entitles them to walk into a corner office.

Understanding why Millennials think they can change the world will help managers change their companies for the better. The notion that young professionals are entitled is the most common perception of Millennials today; however, it is the myth that managers can use most easily to find the motivating factor unique to young employees.

FACT 1: MILLENNIALS HAVE BEEN TOLD A COLLEGE DEGREE EQUALS EMPLOYMENT.

College enrollment tends to be higher during times of economic instability, a trend Millennials have accepted as reality as they come of age[2]. Unlike previous generations, many Millennials had college presented not just as an option but also as an expectation.

From high school classrooms to today's highly educated culture, Millennials understand that if they want a "good-paying job," whatever that means, they need to go to college. If they want to be competitive, they should plan on attending graduate school as well.

From an early age, we learn that doing well in elementary and middle school will set a solid foundation for success in high school. As we get older, we jump into math clubs, lacrosse teams, and violin lessons to boost our competitive edge over our peers when it comes time for college applications. SAT coaches and college consultants are in high demand to help anxious students and parents make the best possible decision for a successful future.

As college students, we float amongst majors to find the most viable and interesting course of study possible. For four-plus years, we are consumed with writing term papers late into the night and cramming for finals early in the morning. The content of what is learned or taught is not as important as the certificate of proof itself. In fact, many of us assume just attending class warrants at least a C (maybe even a B if we are on time).

After 16-plus years in the classroom and thousands of dollars in debt, we graduate, hopeful that a little piece of paper (also known as a college degree) will finally turn into something useful, allowing us to attain our ultimate goal: a job.

THE MILLENNIAL AMERICAN DREAM

The problem with this system is that no one is setting expectations for these twenty-somethings fresh out of college. The Millennial version of the American dream is "work hard in school today, get offered an awesome job tomorrow." Young students look forward to achieving this dream as the prize for their hard work, but no one ever explained it to them in real terms. So now these fresh-faced Millennials are walking into their first day on the job and are hit with the all-too-real reality of work.

I finished undergrad in 2009 with no debt, but also no job. When my bank account hit 62 cents, my mother's couch became surprisingly less comfortable; I began working for a consulting company with a downtown office and a long list of newsworthy clients.

My first day, I walked into the beautiful building illuminated by skylights and pictured myself in meetings, making presentations to clients, and multi-tasking while on conference calls. I had no idea what I would be doing or saying in any of these situations, but it all seemed so glamorous and mature.

I introduced myself to the secretary and she asked me to follow her back to where my office was. A real office! Most of my friends were pouring espresso and I had a legitimate office! Visions of bookcases and leather chairs were dancing in my head as we turned down the hallway; the secretary pointed to the door by a blue recycle bin. As I opened the door, the smell of detergent filled the air. In what appeared to be a newly converted cleaning closet sat a computer desk, laptop, and filing cabinet. I would have to hold off on the leather couch, but at least I had a four walls and a door.

Six months passed. I was having coffee with my undergraduate advisor one day when I asked, "Is this really all there is? Do people really work eight hours a day, five days a week for the rest of their lives?"

It had seemed so glorious in my head: drinking coffee in business meetings, conference-calling during my commute, and carrying a company credit card. But as Millennials like myself are waking up, they are finding that reality is often far different than the dream.

HARD WORK IS HARD WORK

Millennials have inherited a terrible economy. The average college senior who graduated in 2011 was $26,600 in debt. Even our parents mortgaged their homes, took out loans, and deferred retirement so we could attend the best schools their money could buy. It's hard to build a career when you're digging out of a massive debt-hole. Millennials have been sold a bag of goods that no one can deliver on: certainty. We have had to fight for jobs, even at the most entry-level, competing with people of all ages and levels of experience.

FACT 2: MILLENNIALS HAVE HAD HIGH EXPECTATIONS SET FOR THEM SINCE BIRTH.

Millennials have been given the title the "look at me" generation, implying that they are self-obsessed, over-confident, and arrogant. Those same cute little toddlers crying "look at me" to cooing parents as they took their first steps have continued to have their hands held as they walked into homeroom and finally, into the boardroom. One manager interviewed mentioned his Millennials would expect praise after turning in expense reports on time. His response: "This isn't T-ball!"

We have had the rules changed in our favor nearly our entire lives. If we didn't like our grades, Mom and Dad called our teachers. If we weren't playing enough during the game, Mom and Dad pulled the coach aside.

So now we are faced with the brave new world of employment where the rules aren't bent in our favor. Mom and Dad can't make a call. Rules can't be changed. And for the first time for many of us, we are feeling an overwhelming sense of disappointment and failure. Not only that, we have to explain to parents who were screaming on the soccer sidelines why their $60,000 investment can't find a job that doesn't require an apron.

"Parents often talk about the younger generation as if they didn't have anything to do with it."
Haim Ginott, author of *Parent and Child*

Our Boomer parents are notorious for being helicopter parents. This has proven to be both a blessing and a handicap for their children. We have experienced sheltered childhoods complete with baby-gates and parent-teacher nights. We have come of age comfortable with parents intervening in our lives. We have been told from a young age how "special" and "unique" we are.

THE NEXT GREATEST GENERATION?

In their foundational book, *Generations,* sociologists William Strauss and Neil Howe identify Millennials as the next "Hero Generation," mimicking the generational personality-type of the Greatest Generation. They write,

> Whatever practical agenda comes their way, Millennials will figure out a solution, organize, cooperate, share burdens, and get the job done—all with an effectiveness and cheerfulness that will stun their elders...Assuming the crisis turns out well, Millennials will forever be honored as a generation of civic achievers.[3]

No pressure.

Expert motivator Jim Rohn explained, "Children will do great things when they have great things to do." Having high levels of expectations set for us is important because we need to be believed in, challenged, and encouraged.

TWO CHALLENGES YOU NEED TO GET OVER

In light of these facts, here are two distinct challenges managers face:

1. Be careful to set realistic expectations.

It is dangerous to set unrealistic expectations for a group of teenagers and twenty-somethings before they figure out who they are as individuals—let alone as a generation! That means not over-projecting our abilities, but also, not underestimating what we can do. If you ask Millennials, we will be honest about where we are and what we are comfortable with taking on. We don't want to let down our bosses or, ourselves, and are terrified of not achieving our dreams.

In the meantime, we are having our goals set by our parents, bosses, and professors. It's not helpful when managers project expectations that are beyond our expertise or experience. We may not be able to achieve them. Instead, it's better for managers to view themselves as coaches assessing our abilities while pushing us to attain our full capacity. We are a work in progress, and we need help to fulfill our potential.

2. *Share that recognition takes sacrifice.*

Many young people confuse expectations with achievement and want the recognition without the sacrifice. Millennials may get so addicted to acknowledgment and positive feedback that they might come to expect it without putting forth the effort to earn it. This only teaches us that we can get whatever we want without hard work. We would be wise to remember the Greatest Generation only earned their name after they survived world war and the Great Depression.

RECOGNITION IS A POWERFUL MOTIVATOR

If someone believes you can do something, it feels almost as good as actually achieving it. We see this particularly with volunteerism amongst Millennials. Naturally, it feels good to volunteer at an animal shelter or a nature preserve; but it feels even better when we post pictures of it on Facebook and get recognition for our good deeds from our social network, whether or not we actually planted a tree or rescued a puppy.

As the "Hero Generation," we want our work to make a difference in the world and have higher meaning. Plus, we have been told that we can and will change the world. Our sense of self-worth is naturally questioned when we find ourselves pouring coffee or filing depositions. We went to college to learn how to make the world a better place, not to sit on the sidelines of history.

Managers can use the Millennial need for recognition as a motivator on the job. "Employee of the Month" may be a cheesy and somewhat outdated practice, but there is a reason it has been around so long—it works! Praising hardworking staff members by highlighting their contributions encourages all employees to work harder. That could be as simple as sending around an email featuring one of the new associates, asking the intern to give the update on her project in a staff meeting, or holding a "good deeds and gratitude" raffle.

FACT 3: MILLENNIALS ARE USED TO BEING MARKETED TO.

Remember the highly successful Burger King campaign in the 90's whose slogan was, "Have it your way?" No longer just relevant to someone's choice of condiments, the idea of having it "your way" has emboldened a generation to customize everything from their iPhone accessories to the way they watch television.

Take social media. Facebook started as a way to connect co-eds, but now provides a personalized webpage for millions around the world to present themselves in the most flattering light possible. Thanks to Twitter and Instagram, we can post musings great or small as well as share our lives through photos—making even the most mundane day seem like an adventure. Now even watching television online is an interactive and personalized experience, with each ad catering to the viewer based on his or her preferences and Google search history.

Studies also show that Millennials tend to move and act in large blocks. Not only are we the largest generation in American history, we make similar purchases, vote for similar candidates, and watch similar shows on the Internet (one-in-five of us does not have television service because we consider it wasteful).[4] Sensing our immense purchasing power, industries are responding accordingly, hoping to capitalize on our numbers and disposable incomes.

EDUCATION CHANGED US

Universities are also changing. Online education and flexible class schedules are keeping higher education institutions competitive. Some are creating niche courses designed to attract Millennials' diverse interests, even offering classes on Lady Gaga and home brewing (though hopefully not together!).

We don't like buying textbooks, so we created an industry to rent them. We trust our friends' opinions above those of the experts, so we rate our professors online. From our earliest days of education, we have managed the way we learn and provided feedback on what works for us, including the use of video games, television, and the internet.

Now we are looking for jobs and are interviewing our prospective employers as much as they are interviewing us. If we feel that our uniqueness is not celebrated, we will pack up and move on.

GENERATIONAL GPS

Millennials are not as "entitled" as they are misdirected. We volunteer to take on more responsibility than is appropriate and have inflated expectations that are not grounded in reality. We take an approach that asks, "If not us, then who?"

We are excited about life because we want to play a prominent role in building a better world. We are ambitious. Our confidence in what we want to do often overshadows the reality of what we *can* do. We expect to be taken seriously, treated as adults, and used for what we bring to the team. We have been given inflated ideas of who we are and praised for contributions we haven't yet made. But all of these characteristics can be leveraged as motivators to inspire us to apply our passion to your projects.

Speed may be the currency of the Millennial generation, but respect is the currency of the Boomer generation.

CHAPTER ONE SUMMARY

Millennials have been promised that if they just graduate from college, finish graduate school, survive law school, or complete trade school, they will get the job of their dreams.

So we dove into higher education—credit cards first—and are now emerging dripping in debt with no job in sight. We have expected Uncle Sam to make good on his promise to put our hard-earned degrees to work. With the job market still recovering, the Millennial head is swirling with the news that reality is not what it looks like on TV.

We want to be a great generation but can't seem to get past the idea of changing the world, to actually change it. We are used to being told we are special and unique. It's no surprise, then, that we expect the job market to be just as excited about us showing up as our parents, teachers, and coaches have been. The people who have influenced us most have set a high bar for us and we are nervous about letting the world down.

As the second largest generation in American history, we have been able to sway the market in our favor—simply with our purchasing power. In our short lives, we have already played a major role in reshaping American social norms, including how we network, earn degrees, and even vote. Now on the job, we volunteer to apply our Millennial expertise to everything from organizational improvements, to marketing plans, to office furniture configuration.

What may seem like entitlement is really ambition that needs some direction. Our excitement about our futures and confidence in our dreams is well intentioned, although sometimes unrealistic. Overcoming the entitlement myth is the first hurdle to helping Millennials "clock in" to life as adults and realize just how they can earn the respect and appreciation they desire from their older colleagues.

TIPS FOR MANAGERS

- *Set clear, realistic expectations.*

  Help Millennials understand what is expected of them and how they can achieve it. We have been trained on course rubrics that outlined what was to be done, when it was due, and how it would be graded. We do well when we have a clear outline of what we need to accomplish. Create project calendars that mimic academic syllabi for younger employees, providing hard deadlines and check-in dates moving them toward the end goal. Institute a shared calendar that allows you to track what parts of the project are being accomplished and when.

  Parents can help their Millennial children prepare for the reality of work by teaching them about the importance of hard work. Managers can help their Millennial employees avoid frustration and lack of motivation by helping them connect their daily tasks to a goal larger than their current position.

- *Clone yourself.*

  As a manager, you only have so many hours in the day. By rewarding ambitious Millennials with mini-manager roles, you will be able to hone their drive, tackle outlier projects, and identify future leaders. It may take some oversight and guidance on the front end, but it will free you up to handle your other responsibilities.

- *Go ahead, feed their egos.*

  Studies show that when individuals believe they are better at a sport, they actually perform better.[5] Telling your Millennial employees that they are incredible writers, gifted communicators, or natural networkers is not going to cause their egos to burst. It will actually deepen their loyalty to you. Millennials want to know their manager sees their unique talents and that they are naturally good at something.

  Do not, however, give your Millennial employee a compliment that is undeserved. This will only reinforce the negative mindset in which so many Millennials believe they can be the best—effortlessly.

  Despite our collective confidence, we are insecure in our performance on the job and are second-guessing how we act and present ourselves. Focus on encouraging work practices that benefit us and the company.

- ***Reward the small things.***

  Not all of your Millennial employees will walk in on the first day and expect to run the company in five years, but it happens. For those employees itching for a promotion, create mini-rewards for their contributions to the company as a whole. Teach them the importance of hard work and dedication by giving them targets to aim for. Both personal and missional ambition is a powerful thing. Be careful not to crush their spirits. Instead, find or create unique outlets to harness it.

- ***Give them a seat at the table.***

  Help Millennials see how their opinion matters by asking them for it. It seems like such a simple task, but is too often overlooked. When surveyed, one CEO said that when his company was deliberating about whether or not to bring on a client, he turned and asked the intern, "What do you think we should do?" In this instance the CEO agreed and moved on the intern's suggestion. Even if their opinion is not particularly profound, including them as adults in the conversation will help them feel significant and appreciated.

TIPS FOR MILLENNIALS

- *Learning doesn't end in the classroom.*

  Entitlement is the largest challenge you will face when entering the workforce. Make a conscious effort to convince your employer that the number one thing you are confident in is your ability to learn and improve. Be teachable and express a sense of gratitude in your work. Your ability to admit you don't know the answer will demonstrate humility that will build rapport with your boss.

  Here is a good rule of thumb when you are new at the job: it is always better to ask for permission than forgiveness.

- *Counteract every negative with a positive.*

  You may think you can do a better job at certain tasks than your manager. Maybe he or she is terrible at one or more aspects of the job—like returning any of your past seven emails. But no matter what the situation, respect the time and experience of those who are in authority over you.

  Every time you feel yourself getting negative, focus on at least one positive characteristic or thing you can learn from your boss. Ask your manager out to lunch to pick his or her brain on a project, or consult with a more experienced colleague on how he or she has become successful in the company.

- *Stop complaining about the economy.*

  It has hit everyone hard. If you are employed, happily or otherwise, be grateful. There are many who would rather be in your position than stressing about how to pay rent.

- *Get real.*

  Identify your own level of expectation when you enter your new position. Are you being realistic? Do you need to adjust your timeline for advancement based on the present situation? Remember that your older colleagues may have had to work harder and longer to get to where they are. Some of them may even resent you. Go out of your way to show them you value their opinion and respect their work.

CHAPTER 2
MYTH 2: MILLENNIALS ARE DISLOYAL

As a manager for over three decades, Greg has learned the hard way to hire slow, fire fast. After two months of interviews, he has recently brought on Madison, an English graduate student, to work as an editor on the communications team. She seems like the perfect fit for the company culture and has all of the prospects of being a long-term employee.

After one month, Greg begins sending Madison to editors' conferences and writing workshops. He views his recent hire as a long-term investment and wants her to gain the skills necessary to improve her contribution, both to the department and company as a whole.

When she is first hired, Madison isn't definite about her future plans, but she has expressed in the interview an interest in staying with the company after she finishes her studies. Madison seems very content with her role, responds quickly to deadlines, and quietly and skillfully fulfills all of her duties. Everything seems on track until May when she puts in her notice. Madison had been offered a job in public relations and figures it is an opportunity to try something completely new.

"I wasn't aware that you were even interested in public relations. Were you not happy here?" Greg tries to not make it sound personal, but he has put a lot of time and money into his young employee; with her leaving after eight months, it seems like a complete waste.

Trying to explain to Greg that switching careers just sounded like a good idea isn't going over well with her Xer manager. Madison considered the security of her current position, and with the current job market it makes sense to stay. But there is something inside her making her ignore the voice asking, "Why leave?" to go with the voice asking, "Why not?"

IT'S LIKE DATING...

As Millennials, we approach our new jobs like a first date, something fun, exciting and abounding with mystery. We enjoy discovering the unknown, getting to know the position, and playing out in our heads what our futures look like together.

But then we get bored. We talk to our friends. They seem to have better opportunities, more fun, higher pay, and a more attractive future. So we move on and the trend continues.

This generation has dreams of grandeur and can get frustrated with the limitations of holding one job at a time. For our parents, starting a job was like getting married. It was a serious relationship spanning decades. Despite the ups and downs, they endured working late nights and skipping vacations, believing it would be worth it in the end. As the children of workaholic parents, Millennials are starting their own careers wanting something different.

While there is some research claiming Millennial workers are loyal today[6], there is substantial data to suggest that the same worker is twice as likely to leave a company within one year of hire.[7]

So, what causes Millennials to leave a company—and what you can do about it?

1. It depends on the position.

If you see great potential in your Millennial employee and want to keep him or her around long-term, say so. Do not assume that entry-level employees will be content in the same role with your company in five years. Learn more about the career trajectory they envision for themselves by having them fill out a career-map or vision board. What is their "dream job" and what aspects about it (the pay, flexibility, exposure, etc.) are most exciting to them? You can then work to incorporate those aspects into their current and future role in your company.

If you are experiencing a high turnover of Millennials in your mid-level positions, there may be something in your company culture not suitable to the Millennial pallet. Answering these questions may help you discover common themes and motivators amongst your young talent:

- Are their responsibilities on the job more, less, or different than what they were hired to do?

- Do they get a high degree of satisfaction from their work?

- Does your hiring process need to be revised to ensure you are hiring the right talent for the job?

2. It depends on the industry.

Millennials are not as concerned with a traditional career trajectory; although the current job market is slowing us down and keeping us put longer. Industries with the highest Millennial employment are high-tech start-ups and nonprofit organizations.[8] What these careers lack in terms of stability, they make up with unique opportunities, skill attainment, and leadership experience. As a generation who wants to leave our fingerprints on the world, our eyes sparkle with the chance to invest our untapped skills in building something great.

These industries are also notorious for high levels of failure and employee burnout. Working twelve-hour days can only be sustained for so long; like Xers, Millennials prioritize work-life balance more so than their predecessors. If the decision comes between a higher paying (but more exhausting) position and a lower-paying one with more time for travel, studies show that Millennials will take the latter.[9]

This leaves us with these takeaways:

- Don't lose hope if you aren't a young or small company. You can still appeal to the Millennial fascination with starting projects and building programs from the ground up. Incorporate markers for achievement into their current roles and help Millennials plot their own career trajectory within your organization.

- Millennials love a challenge. We are thrilled by the idea of working toward the next goal—be it a raise, more responsibilities, or even a new title. It's up to you to demonstrate that our advancement possibilities within the company are a personal success ladder complete with immediate and long-term career fulfillment.

3. It depends on your own level of expectation.

The hiring process should include an honest conversation about what the working relationship looks like between employee and employer. Include a discussion on reporting including who your new hires will report to and at what frequency (hourly, daily, weekly). Explain how your company measures success and what markers for achievement lead to more responsibility and higher pay. It may seem unnecessary to explain to a new employee what his or her terms of hire are, but unfortunately many Millennials new on the job are clueless as to what is expected of them.

One manager raised her hand at a recent business conference and asked, "Do I really have to be that simplistic with my Millennial employees? Isn't this all just common sense?"

Common sense is relative. Getting a real job for Millennials is like traveling out of the country for the first time. They are clueless as to the customs, language, and culture of their new work environment. Consistently communicating expectations will help both you and your young employees have a more successful and fulfilling workday.

4. Evaluate your expectations:

- What are you looking for from your employees in six months? What about in six years?

- Could some employees ascend into senior leadership positions? If so, help them visualize themselves a few years out.
    o What will they be doing?
    o How will they be challenged?

- Turn the question around on them.
    o What new responsibilities will they want to have?

    ○ How do they plan on contributing to the company's overall goals?

- Revisit vision-casting conversations with your employees regularly. Is there flexibility within the role or do you need experts in one particular field?

A sure way to keep your Millennial employee longer than the typical two-year turnaround is to establish a vision match between candidates and the company. Determine if the individual is a fit for the company culture before deciding if he or she is a fit for the position.

FACT 1: MILLENNIALS COMMIT TO PEOPLE, NOT COMPANIES.

Studies show that the Millennial generation is fiercely loyal.[10] However our generational loyalty is reactive, rather than proactive. We reserve our allegiance for those who have made a personal investment in our lives and generally commit to individuals, not organizations. Institutions such as charitable nonprofits and universities tend to be the exception to this trend.

We crave genuine relationships and stay connected with teachers, coaches, and mentors who positively impact our lives when we are young. We are a generation that is incredibly mobile, moving from state-to-state and sometimes country-to-country in search of life experience. Thanks to technology, we can stay constantly connected to those vast networks and maintain strong bonds no matter the distance.

In his book, *Bowling Alone: The collapse and revival of the American community*, Robert Putnam explains this phenomenon of disassociation across all generations. "What really matters from the point of view of social capital and civic engagement is not merely nominal membership, but active and involved membership."[11]

PUT YOURSELF ON THEIR TEAM

Before they develop intense loyalty to others, Millennials first have to feel invested in. Managers can win a place in the Millennial heart, but it will take some work. By positioning themselves as not only "bosses" but as coaches and mentors, managers will allow Millennials to engage with them and commit the most valuable commodity they have—time—to do what their managers ask of them.

Millennials tend to blur the lines between their personal and professional worlds. They feel comfortable discussing their love interests and personal ambitions with customers and coworkers—even when it isn't appropriate. Still, by taking a reasonable interest in their lives outside of work, managers will help build the trust Millennials are looking for in their professional roles.

FACT 2: MILLENNIALS HAVE A FEAR OF BEING BORED.

Boredom. It's the number one reason young people drop out of school according to a recent survey.[12] Most Millennials aren't ditching class because illegal activity is more appealing or access to classes is too difficult.

We leave because we don't see a practical reason for spending eight hours a day sitting at a desk not learning anything relevant.

CREATE AN ENGAGING ENVIRONMENT

As Millennials, we are accustomed to being entertained everywhere. (Even my dentist has a little television screen for me to watch while I'm having my teeth cleaned.) No need to install an entertainment system for your employees or place a popcorn machine in the break room (but who doesn't love popcorn?). A proven tactic to keep employees is creating a work environment that stimulates the human imagination.

Don't worry if you are clueless as to how to liven up your office culture. Commission a multi-generational group of creative and ambitious employees to brainstorm ideas on how everyone can enjoy a more engaging and stimulating work environment.

Millennials do not want to be treated like cogs in a wheel. We have been told our entire lives how special and unique we are. Placing us in a fluorescent-lit room with identical cubicles will only feed into the fear that we are just like everyone else.

An office environment should reflect the personality of the company and project the confidence and excellence you desire each of your employees to possess. We take a lot of pride in our work settings. Give us something to brag about—even if it is as simple as putting a vision board in the break room or painting a wall bright green in the office. Keep things moving for us and we will keep things moving for you.

FACT 3: MILLENNIALS ARE RECOVERING INTERNS.

Visit any career office on a college campus and it will not take long to find a nearly endless list of intern and fellowship opportunities. Most undergraduate programs require an internship of some sort, and many universities even offer classes to help students perfect the art of interning.

Internships allow Millennials to test out career fields and positions within organizations without the commitment of being hired as full-time employees. It exposes them to various industries they may not have known anything about and diversifies their portfolio of understanding.

I am not bashing internships—the three internships and two fellowships that I have participated in significantly shaped my career. However, there is a growing tendency for Millennials to get stuck in the revolving door of internships (partially due to the economy) and never grow up into full-fledged employees.

For all of the intrinsic benefits of interning, it also feeds the Millennial aversion to commitment. Whether it is committing to another person or committing to use the same smartphone for a year, this generation does not want to get locked into anything. When we encourage a culture of internships, we teach Millennials to hop from one position to the next, pick up whatever relevant skills they can, then hop along to the next opportunity.

Many young people are being hired right out of school and maintaining the same responsibilities as when they were interns, but with a paycheck. As we will discuss in the last chapter, money is not the only motivator for Millennials. We want responsibility and influence within the organization that goes beyond what we did as the unpaid help in college.

GENERATIONAL ROI

Like any relationship, there is an investment of time required to build rapport and loyalty with young employees. The return on investment will be worth it.

Millennials will invest in you when you invest in them.

When you are able to establish genuine relationships with Millennials, you will infuse creativity and passion into their work and unlock skills and talents you never knew they had.

CHAPTER TWO SUMMARY

It seems that Millennials have evolved into a generation addicted to change. We want things to move quickly, be user-friendly and keep us entertained at all times. Millennials have a fear that if we stand still for too long, we will start to actually move backwards.

Constantly moving forward and leap-frogging from one job to the next has somehow become associated with upward mobility in our minds. But it has also earned us the reputation of being disloyal.

We are a generation afraid to commit because we don't want to miss out on a better alternative—even if something better never comes along. When we do commit, we are loyal to people over organizational structures. We want whoever we work for to mentor and coach us, and we crave human interaction with those in company leadership.

Managers can mitigate the Millennial flight by adopting the characteristics of industries and organizations that Millennials are most attracted to. Primarily, Millennnials want to feel needed and put on a team that appreciates their unique contributions. When we feel that our colleagues, our bosses, and our organizations are proud of us, we will be proud of them (and are in no way shy about sharing it— Hello, status updates!). You will see a generation of individuals exuding a new pride and confidence in their work, and exhibiting a commitment to their company and fierce loyalty to you as their manager.

TIPS FOR MANAGERS

* *Create a space that iWorks.*

    Millennials have instant buy-in when they are a part
    of putting something together. When their
    workspace reflects their personality, Millennials
    feel an instant connection with the company as a
    whole. Even something as simple as allowing them
    to pick out their own office chair (extra points if
    there are different color options) or encouraging
    them to personalize their work space, will help them
    feel more at home. Ask a group of creative
    employees to brainstorm ideas on "brightening" up
    the office in a way that energizes and engages
    employees.

* *Map out their goals.*

    Within the first month of employment, ask
    Millennials to explain their unique contribution to
    the company. Most managers hand an employee a
    job description and leave it at that. People, like
    positions, are not one-size-fits-all. Make the
    conversation two-way when discussing what your
    employees will be contributing. Ask them to
    seriously consider what opportunities they want to
    pursue in the future and then help them map out
    how they can get there.

After about two months, have your employees write out how they see their own responsibilities and roles growing within the company in the next three to five years. By putting proverbial pen to paper, Millennials will be able to visualize themselves with your organization longer than the typical two-year stint. Millennials are still on the semester system, so it is important to revisit these goals every six months.

- *Find mission alignment.*

Counteract the Millennial aversion to organizational loyalty by finding opportunities to reinforce how the company's mission and each of your employees' personal missions align. Ask your employees to write out how they uniquely see themselves in the company's vision/mission statement and share these statements across the staff.

Take time to have top leadership touch base with newer employees to eliminate the distance between top decision makers and decision implementers, even if that means having executives take a walk through the cubicle neighborhood or committing to email one new employee a week. Accessibility is important to Millennials because it leads to meaningful relationships.

- *Don't take it personally.*

If, and when, Millennials do leave, don't take it personally. Deciding on a career—let alone starting one—can be incredibly stressful. If you remember being in your twenties, odds are that you didn't have it all figured out either. Be gracious and be understanding, even if you don't understand.

- *Lay it out on the table.*

Having both sides be open about what they expect a role to look like will help the employee and employer have a more fulfilling employment experience. Ask your Millennial what they would like to learn in this position, as well as what they plan to contribute. Have management do the same. For a generation afraid of commitment and "missing out," Millennials will thrive with the assurance and security of knowing what is expected of them. If they are unsure, encourage them to come to you with questions.

TIPS FOR MILLENNIALS

- *Be honest.*

In your interview explain how you are committed to the mission of the organization you are applying for. Use discernment but be honest about how long you plan on staying with the company. Some managers expect you to stay in the position for only a year. Others may see you taking over their responsibilities in five years so they can retire. Management is making an investment of time and resources in you and deserves to know your level of commitment.

- *What doesn't kill you will make you stronger.*

When you don't land the job, inquire about why the company doesn't see you as a fit. Use each opportunity to strengthen your skillset and expand your network. The manager will respect you for taking the process of applying for jobs seriously and it will serve as a learning experience for you.

- *Do your duty.*

Motivational giant Jim Rohn once said, "Some people plant in the spring and leave in the summer. If you've signed up for a season, see it through. You don't have to stay forever, but at least stay until you see it through." If you aren't feeling fulfilled or even appreciated at your job now, do your duties at work and be faithful to do what is expected of you until it is appropriate to move on.

- *Slow your roll.*

If you are getting the 12-month itch, stop and reflect. What is making you want to move on? Is it the pay, the people, the work environment, or the position? Most factors, apart from the organization's mission, are in your sphere of influence. Ask for a raise or promotion of responsibilities if appropriate. See about a role rotation within the company to work with other groups or tackling different projects. Diversify your responsibilities if you feel yourself feeling stagnant. It is not your boss's responsibility to keep you occupied. .

BONUS: FREE GUIDE TO HIRING MILLENNIALS

Discover the perfect questions to ask in the interview, the websites to recruit from and techniques for onboarding America's largest generation.

www.hiringguide.millennialsolution.com

CHAPTER 3
MYTH 3: MILLENNIALS ARE INDEPENDENT

Robert has just taken the helm of a small real estate firm bleeding profit, despite being in one of the largest and fastest-growing markets.

Walking into the office, he immediately notices a clear distinction between senior management and lower-level employees. Company leadership tends to leave the office for lunch while younger employees bring their lunches and sit at the conference table. There is hardly any interaction between the two groups apart from tasking out projects and reporting on results.

When the team misses a project deadline for a bread-and-butter client, Robert decides that something has to be done. The entire staff is capable, responsible, and intelligent. In its early days, the company has seen rapid growth but as it has gotten larger and more diverse, its competitive edge has dulled. It's like Robert has all of the parts to build a Swiss watch—he just needs to get the right gears, switches, and cogs in place.

After surveying his staff, Robert discovers the largest challenge is the chasm in communication between the higher-ups and his account managers. The two operate nearly independent of one another. Management considers younger staff to be cliquish and prone to groupthink. Whenever the junior employees are asked their opinion, they look at their friends and colleagues for an answer. When asked, young employees share they are intimidated when asking questions and feel more like "gophers" in the office than contributing members of the group.

Robert tries an experiment in which he breaks up teams into groups based on the geographic area they cover, rather than by years of experience. Sofia, who has just joined the company last month, is on the same team as Hugh, a senior-level manager who has been with the company since the beginning.

It isn't long before Robert notices the barriers between staff begin to break down and more creative ideas come to the forefront. Hugh has no idea that Sofia has spent her childhood in the area he covered; through their initial conversation, they both learn he has actually sold her family their first home. By interacting with more experienced staff, Sofia learns how her work in the office helps to transform people's lives—including families like her own—and decides to begin studying for her real estate license.

What started as a company structure based on bureaucratic processes and titles has now become a family-style work environment where staff members—no matter their experience—collaborate on projects to get them done with excellence. Robert has taken a challenge that once seemed nearly impossible and created opportunity for cross-generational teamwork and relationship building.

THE MILLENNIAL GENERATIONAL IDENTITY

It is human nature to self-associate with individuals who affirm who we are. No one has to tell a kindergartner to only make friends with the little girls or little boys he likes; he just does it without thinking. The same principles that apply on the playground also apply to the trading floor. However, just because young employees cluster together like middle-schoolers at their lockers, does not mean that they prefer the company of their cohort over the companionship of older colleagues.

Millennials recognize that they are entering adulthood at a different pace than those who have gone before them. Many of us will start our first job at the same age our parents and grandparents were having their first children. Our collective experience has come to define us as late-bloomers and codependent. This has created a generational stereotype unique to us, similar to the quintessential straight-laced teens of the 50's, the cultural rebels of the 60's and 70's, and the grungy young adults of the 90's. In fact, nine out of ten of us agree that the Millennial generation shares "specific beliefs, attitude and experiences" that uniquely set us apart from other generations.[13]

Working in a small office, I was the only one who wasn't pregnant or raising a small child. My coworkers would come in exhausted after being up all night with their babies; I came in exhausted from staying out with my friends. They spent their money on new furniture for their track houses; I spent my money on books for grad school...and shoes. They shared recipes and brought muffins to work; I was surviving off of cereal.

Although there was little about them I could personally relate to, my coworkers made me feel included in the nuances of their lives. This brought me closer to my colleagues as friends and work associates. Here, I had a whole group of young parents who were serving as role models on how to balance caring for young children with a rising career. They shared with me their victories and also their defeats, making tough but heroic decisions to put their families first. If they had assumed that my age and experience distanced me from being relevant in their conversation, I would have been deprived of the distinct pleasure of getting to learn and grow through their life experiences.

When work environments are segregated along the lines of race, age, gender, or experience, the company and its staff suffer. Not only does a culture of inclusion and collaboration improve productivity when executed correctly, it also positively affects the personal lives of everyone on the team. Human society cannot survive without multiple age groups sharing knowledge and experience, and neither can our workplaces.

FACT 1: MILLENNIALS ARE NATURAL TEAM PLAYERS.

Millennials are a generation of recovering little league stars and soccer team drop-outs. Nearly all of us played organized sports (whether we wanted to or not) and are used to working with others toward a shared goal. From an early age, we have been conditioned to develop an affinity for playing off of the strengths of our teammates. We learned early on that it feels better to win than to lose— although we would probably get a trophy either way.

Coaches and professors alike have drilled into the Millennial mind that working well on a team today is the ticket to professional success tomorrow. Millennials have learned to measure individual success by collective achievement. We heard it everywhere from classroom posters declaring, "There is no 'I' in 'Team'" to popular movies like *The Mighty Ducks*. Our childhood hero Michael Jordan even taught us, "Talent wins games, but teamwork and intelligence wins championships."

Millennials gain validation from interacting with peers and managers alike. It is not just a phenomenon on Facebook to "like" the activity of fellow users; if we had our way, we would install "like" buttons and status updates on our progress reports, PowerPoint presentations, and year-end summaries.

MILLENNIALS LOVE TEAMS

Not only do teams provide a sense of structured nostalgia for Millennials, studies show Millennials find excessive comfort in team-based direction, oversight and decision-making. We walk into a new job and immediately begin looking for a peer group. We have a need to feel instantly and constantly connected to others. Consider the last family reunion you went to; any teenage Millennial not being engaged with others was most likely on his or her phone—texting, browsing the internet, or checking in on social media. The threat of isolation is terrifying to Millennials.

Although there is decentralized authority within a group, there is also a higher level of involvement. In a group, we have control over how much or how little we bring to the table. This is important for a generation of people inspired by a sense of contribution, knowing they played a role—no matter how small—in something bigger than themselves.

Millennials are also prone to gravitate toward group work because there is built in anonymity. When you are one of many, it is easier to avoid the risk associated with independent action if the project goes poorly. When asked in an interview whether they prefer independent or group work, most Millennials will have an identical answer: both. Many, though not all, Millennials thrive when working independently. We enjoy being given a task and feeling the satisfaction of knowing we accomplished the task on our own. However, we have also grown up in a culture where our success—be it a grade or a championship—depends on the collective success of everyone.

THE MILLENNIAL DIFFERENCE ON TEAMS

A mini-experiment was conducted to study how teams comprised of different ages respond to project management. Four younger employees were placed in one group and four older employees in another. Each team was tasked with building a snowman.

The Millennials quickly fell into traditional group roles with a single administrator and multiple executors. The members of that group discussed the collective vision of what the snowman would look like much less than the role each person would play in completing the project. After a few minutes of deliberating, one member volunteered to gather the firewood, another designed the mittens, and another started balling the cold snow up to make up the body.

The older employees with more leadership experience took significantly more time deciding who took on what role. They were concerned with what the snowman was going to look like, how tall it was going to be, and—most importantly—what its purpose was.

The Millennials thrived on the spontaneity and mystery of what their snowman would actually look like. The end product for them, in this case a snowman, was not nearly as important as the process of getting there. Although it took longer to build the snowman, members of the younger group expressed higher levels of satisfaction and collaboration than the older, seemingly more efficient group.

This exercise works well with short-term projects like the example included here. However, projects spanning a longer timeframe tend to see Millennial dissolution if no one provides clear priorities and mile-markers. If the task was to make snowmen for the next six months, we may have found our more seasoned team working together more efficiently because of their more clearly defined roles.

Unlocking the Millennial power of teamwork comes with its own set of challenges. Many Millennials have learned to "go along to get along" and fall into traditional group roles when there is a strong leader. Managers can mitigate this by constructing intentional teams with a diverse range of skills, ages, and expertise.

Managers can also help the team be successful by ensuring each member is given clear and appropriate tasks and held accountable for his or her contribution to the group. They can encourage team members to self-evaluate and even offer incentives for consistently contributing to the group's overall success.

As authors Lynn Lancaster and David Stillman write in *The M Factor: How the Millennial Generation Is Rocking the*

Workplace, "While Xers saw independence as strength, Millennials see collaboration as power."[14]

FACT 2: MILLENNIALS CRAVE MENTORS.

Learning to lead is a high priority for Millennials. We are a generation longing for prominent positions but unprepared at present to take them. According to *Keeping the Millennials: Why Companies Are Losing Billions in Turnover to This Generation- and What to Do About It*, "Millennials come to the workplace with education and rich learning experiences from their youth, but they haven't always been schooled in the skills necessary to lead others."[15]

We consider ourselves leaders, but most of us have no concept of what that means. Our heroes include Steve Jobs, Jay-Z, and Oprah. We idolize self-made men and women who created a name for themselves despite great difficulty and challenge. We respect renaissance men and women who are specialists across multiple fields. We want to mimic their rise to fame; however, we are completely clueless as to what it takes to get to the top.

Why leave the nest, when it's so comfortable?

Although eager to be treated as adults, Millennials don't want to be pushed out of the nest too quickly. In 2012, 36 percent of Millennials still lived at home[16]. We still count on the insights and opinions of our parents and, unlike the stereotype of most teenagers, we actually care what our elders think of us.

Many Millennials have a great relationship with their parents—sometimes a little too great. Mom and Dad have given us advice on what topic to research in history class, what instrument to play, what college to go to, and now that we are in the workforce, what job to take.

When presented the option, Millennials are five times more likely than Boomers or Xers to have their parents negotiate their salary or benefits.[17] If you have hired a Millennial in the last five years, odds are they consulted with at least one of their parents during the interview process and heavily relied on their opinion in deciding whether or not to take the job. Companies are now responding in kind to parental involvement. In 2013, Google hosted its second annual, "Take Your Parent to Work Day" at its headquarters in Mountain View, California.

In a 2008 survey, Millennials identified "working with a manager I can respect and learn from" as one of the most important aspects of the work environment"[18] Mentors are incredibly important to in helping Millennials adjust to the new culture of the office. Millennials are naturally inquisitive and want to make sure they do the task right the first time. No doubt new employees will have questions not covered in the employee handbook like, "Can I wear a hoodie if I get cold?" or "Is it appropriate to call the boss by his first name?" These nuanced queries are most appropriately fielded by a patient and accommodating mentor.

Setting up a mentoring program is a simple and cost-effective approach to training and retaining promising staff.

SECRETS TO MENTORING MILLENNIALS

- Assign transitional mentors to help Millennial employees adjust to new roles and greater responsibilities. Ask those who have made a similar transition to give advice and share personal experience as to how they have made the change, and what they would do differently next time.

- Engage younger employees as well. Mentors do not necessarily need to be a 30-year veteran; they could have be on the job three years or even less. Younger employees often make great mentors because they understand the unique challenges that new hires are going through.

- Include a conversation on company culture like traditions, communication patterns, expected work ethic, and other aspects of the new job.

- Ask employees vacating their current position to make a list of "Things I Wish I had Known" to help their replacement get a running start on the job.

- Set clear expectations from both mentor and apprentice including frequency of interaction and measures of success. The clearer the expectations, the more fulfilling and effective the relationship.

- Select mentors based on their willingness to engage in one-on-one interaction with apprentice employees and share insight, advice, challenges, empathy, and candid feedback.

BOSS FOR THE DAY

Have you ever wondered what it would be like to be President for a day? If you only had 24 hours to be the most powerful person in the world, what would you spend it doing? Odds are you would take a different approach to the work than you do at your current day on the job.

Putting yourself in the position of top-dog changes your perspective. When you see things from the top down, you begin to understand the challenges of leadership and the hurdles to success that those who manage you face every day. Consider opportunities to share leadership experiences with young employees.

- Place Millennials in mini-manager positions where they are able to make executive decisions pending manager approval. This will help them practice leadership under pressure, while protecting them against making large-scale mistakes.

- Role-play and help Millennials work through challenges that they will face as managers.

- Ask them who their most effective boss has been. What was it about his or her leadership style and technique that made them so enjoyable to work with?

- Have them identify the three leadership areas with which they are most comfortable (examples include leading small group discussions, taking the lead on ideation, etc.) and three areas in which they need additional training.

Although you may not want to implement a boss-for-a-day program at your office, the principle still applies. Helping employees—particularly new or younger ones—understand the expectations of leadership will give them a newfound dedication to you as a manager and the company as an employer.

Mentoring doesn't mean a massive time commitment and doesn't even require starting a new program. It may look like job shadowing, job rotations across departments, and special assignments like being involved in the orientation process. Be creative!

- Send Millennials to industry-related conferences for ongoing education.

- Encourage younger employees to read management books and attend webinars. Mentors can be virtual as well as conceptual.

- Create peer-mentoring pods. Place employees new to the organization or the position within a group of peers who can help them work through some of the challenges they may be experiencing.

- Connect them with a citywide (or even virtual) young professional group that provides networking and professional development opportunities.

FACT 3: WE'LL ADMIT IT—WE'RE JUST LIKE OUR PARENTS.

It's Saturday night and Jamie is sitting in a smoky jazz club with her friends. Her boyfriend turns to her and says, "I'm so glad your dad told us about this band!" Jamie nods in agreement, pulls out her phone and snaps a photo of the lead guitarist then quickly texts it to her dad three states away.

MILLENNIALS VS PARENTS

In addition to being called Generation Y, iGeneration, and Generation Me, Millennials are also called the Echo-boomers. At first Millennials earned this title because their comparable size to the Boomer generation; however, it now seems even more fitting because they are more like their parents than anyone expected.

Popular media paints the picture of parents and their adult children with a relationship rivaling that of cats and dogs. But reality proves much different.

Millennials and their Boomer parents have parallel personality types, share an affinity for technology, and have a love for personal freedom and not being told what to do. This makes us natural partners in the office, where we can play off of one another's strengths.

Every generation faces an uphill battle as it comes of age. Boomers' bosses didn't take them seriously in their twenties, with their long hair and peace-loving view of life. When members of Generation X entered the workplace, they were stereotyped as out-of-touch Goths, computer whiz kids, or Cher from *Clueless*.

Millennials are transitioning from big-man-on-campus who can do no wrong to office assistant who can't seem to do anything right. We are walking into the work world like a blind date, with high levels of expectation but an inadequate frame of reference. Managers should approach the start of a working relationship with each new employee as a new slate, not letting their past experience with Millennials (negative or positive) impact their immediate impression. Keep in mind the perspective each of us brings to the table includes predispositions encouraged by our upbringing. It's the manager's job to look past the stereotype and see the Millennial employee as an individual and not a statistic.

LEAVING A LEGACY

Human history depends on the successful passage of knowledge and experience to the next generation. Ronald Reagan used to say in his speeches, "Freedom is always one generation away from extinction."

You need us. And we need you. Some of us may act like we know it all, but the reality is that we want to work with you and learn from you. Find opportunities to share your triumphs and challenges to help the next generation of clueless (yet curious) twenty-somethings prepare to take on future leadership in the companies and organizations you lead today.

CHAPTER THREE SUMMARY

Millennials love working in teams. We gain a great deal of satisfaction by problem solving with those of diverse backgrounds. To us, collaboration with those who have other views is a learning experience in itself. The process of hitting the goal is just as important as accomplishing it. This includes the relationships we build along the way; we want to look back and say, "We built that...together."

Teamwork also allows us to specialize in our interest areas. If the group is large enough, then each of us can do exactly what he or she wants—and we can still be successful. The challenge in team-settings is that we have learned what we need to do to get by if we are not personally invested or inspired by the goal of the group.

Despite what most teenagers say, we actually don't think we know it all. Mentoring—whether formal or informal—is very important for us. We want to feel invested in and we long for career and life coaches who see the diamonds in the rough. Company leadership can set up a number of different opportunities to engage the Millennial need for mentoring.

Most Millennials have a positive relationship with their parents. We can relate to their style, musical taste, and even hobbies. This provides a natural on-ramp to building relationships with our Boomer bosses. We want to know that we are the same as others and have been conditioned to be team players for the good of the group. Millennials want to work with others, but are often intimidated by their position and inexperience. We are looking for our organization's leadership to invite us to sit at the table and feel like we are part of something bigger than ourselves.

TIPS FOR MANAGERS

- *Hit the cross-trainer.*

   Train new and young employees across various departments, providing them a holistic view of what the company does. This will help them understand and appreciate what each member of the company contributes as well as providing them an overview of company culture to which they may not be exposed otherwise.

- *Establish a functional mentoring program.*

  Appoint each employee a transitional mentor who will provide timely, empathetic, and insightful feedback as he or she starts his or her new role. Encourage peer-mentoring and mentoring outside the company as well. Make sure to include measures for success and clear expectations for both parties.

- *Build teams intentionally.*

  Allow Millennials to collaborate with their colleagues and others not in their age bracket. Remember, they get their sense of satisfaction from working with others. Encourage team-building exercises that partner individuals of different generations together to solve problems unassociated with work.

- *Give Millennials homework.*

  Ask Millennials about their most effective boss and help them analyze what made this individual so good at his or her job. Have them identify the three areas of leadership in which they are most comfortable (examples include leading small group discussions, taking the lead on ideation, etc.) and three areas in which they need additional training.

TIPS FOR MILLENNIALS

- *Admit when you don't know.*

  Don't be afraid to ask for help, mentoring, or coaching. Asking for help may pertain to a particular project you can't do effectively or successfully on your own. Mentoring involves someone who has been in the same career or position who can lend personal insight to your situation. Coaching may include asking for help from someone outside of your company or industry who can help you gain outside skills to improve your overall performance on and off the job.

- *Be respectful of your elder colleagues.*

  They may not be as excited about working in teams as you are and may even see you as a threat to their own career advancement. Ease into working relationships with coworkers who seem unsure about your role in the company. Share that you respect what they have done and offer yourself as a resource to help them on their next project.

- *Get some perspective.*

Realize that many in older generations are frustrated with Millennials because younger people are taking their jobs. It may not be personal, so practice humility and patience. Great things take time. An effective (or even enjoyable) working relationship may not form until after you work well on a team with others.

• *Ask the right questions.*

Visit The Millennial Solution website at www.millennialsolution.com and explore the resources to find a list of "Questions every Millennial should ask on the job, but are afraid to." This is a good start to being prepared when entering interviews, salary negotiations, and even mentoring meetings.

BONUS: FREE GUIDE TO MENTORING MILLENNIALS

Avoid the most common mistakes leaders make when mentoring, plus discover the best practices for developing a corporate mentoring program.

www.mentoring.millennialsolution.com

CHAPTER 4
MYTH 4: MILLENNIALS ARE ADDICTED TO TECHNOLOGY

Kyle is casually scrolling through his newsfeed on Facebook when the unthinkable happens: his mom sends him a friend request.

He has recently finished college and moved across the country to take a job in New York. His mom explains, "I just want to feel like I am still a part of your life. You are so far away over there!" Kyle concedes and makes a mental note to use extra caution when posting on his wall.

Before long, Kyle's mom isn't just following his whereabouts; she is friends with his friends—and is even commenting on their photos! Although all of Kyle's friends think that it is awesome when his mom "checks in" on social media, Kyle is not necessarily convinced.

Welcome to the new global networking platform. In the 21st century, social networking isn't just for college students anymore. Three-fourths of Millennials may have already created a profile on a social media site, but the fastest growing demographic on social media is the Baby Boomer generation.[19]

Millennials didn't invent the internet, but can't imagine doing anything without it. We are tethered to our smart-phones, learn about world affairs from Twitter, and would rather text "OMW" than call to tell you we're on our way.

CUTTING THE CORD

When was the last time you went wireless? If you are reading this on a computer screen, Kindle, or tablet, odds are that you can hardly remember when you were completely disconnected from technology.

Someone stole my iPhone while I was visiting friends in Lake Tahoe. At first I was completely immobilized. My panic ranged from the reasonable to the absurd. What if there was an avalanche and I was buried under 20 feet of snow? How would my family know I was still alive? How would I get back to my hotel? Where was the nearest Starbucks?

Although my initial reaction was to panic and maybe curl up in a ball under the nearest table, I soon realized how liberating it was not to feel the need to constantly be connected to everyone. Humans have existed for centuries before smartphones and even managed to get some things done in the process. Surely I could find my way home (or at least to an Apple store).

We have become so accustomed to our tech security blanket that we can hardly imagine a world where our phones can't simultaneously tell us the weather forecast, update our inbox, and navigate the shortest route home.

As I write this, I am streaming online radio, updating my Facebook status, checking any one of my five email accounts, and texting friends about our evening plans. Yes, I am a Millennial. On the surface our addiction to technology may be obvious. However, our real relationship with technology is multi-faceted and can be an incredible benefit to your company.

FACT 1: TECHNOLOGY HAS CHANGED THE WAY MILLENNIALS DEFINE "WORK."

Work looks different today than it has in the past.

The workforce itself has even changed, shifting over the last forty years from blue-collar to white-collar. It's then moved from white-collar to open-collar. And now we have what I call a "no-collar" casual office culture. We're not quite at the T-shirt stage, but those tech geniuses in Silicon Valley could be changing that soon.

As technology improves, the modern workplace is being forced to change along with it. Many low-skill jobs are being replaced by high-tech solutions, creating a better quality of life for everyone. A hard day's work for many in older generations included waking up at dawn to milk the cows, walking across the pasture to pump water from the well, and bringing the cattle around before dark.

A hard day's work today may include waking up at three in the morning for a conference call with China, returning emails over lunch, and staying up until two in the morning to redesign a client's website. Starting a business for our parents and grandparents did not include researching wikisites on how to professionally market online for cheap or reading blogs on filing for business status.

In a manufacture-dominant work culture, a successful work day ends in a finished product: a car, a plane, a widget of some kind. In a tech-dominant environment, it can be difficult to measure productivity. Rather than physical products, we have "soft products:" hits on a webpage, email open-rates, graphic design appeal.

Millennials are embracing this trend and loving the flexibility that technology is giving them. We don't want to be constrained by the nine-to-five grind that has defined the work lives of our parents and grandparents. Many of us are coming from college environments where online classes and testing were the norm. We earned our degrees from our couches and didn't even have to show up for class on time.

However, just because we work in our sweats does not mean that we are any less committed to working hard. We consider ourselves just as productive (sometimes even more productive) working from a coffee shop or our living room, as we do in the office.

One Millennial business owner who was surveyed explained, "My clients don't know if I am sending them a report from my desk or the beach. As long as I do my job, I don't think it should matter. The rest is geography."

THE LINE

A blurred line exists between the personal and professional lives of Millennials. Because of technology, we can respond to the boss' email from a barstool or review talking points for a presentation while waiting in line at the grocery store.

Technology allows all of us to bring our two worlds closer than ever before. We rarely leave our work at the office when we walk out for the night and seldom leave our personal lives at the door when we walk in the next morning. Many companies expect employees to be constantly connected and will pay their personal cell phone bills to maintain contact. Checking personal email at work or keeping Facebook open on your desktop is a constant temptation. Some office cultures may be more accepting of employees using office hours to take care of personal errands if they get their work done. But having an open conversation about company policy will help bring clarity for all involved.

In certain industries, there is growing concern that without a structured work environment, Millennials will lack the discipline and focus to get things done. It would be stereotyping to state that all Millennials are more productive at home than at the office. That just simply is not true. The success of flexible working environments depends on the job, just like they depend on the employee/the person. But Millennials today are communicating with their superiors a preference to have the flexibility to take their work with them wherever they go.

When surveying Millennials on this topic, one young worker explained that even if she never did work from home, just having that option available communicated trust from her boss. When a manager gives his or her employee a role in creating an optimal work environment, it tells the employee, and everyone else at the company, that he or she believes in their ability to produce an excellent product without being micro-managed.

Flexibility at work isn't about independence as much as it is about trust. This means a lot for a generation looking to be empowered and believed in.

FACT 2: TECHNOLOGY ACTUALLY MEANS SOMETHING TO MILLENNIALS.

We use technology differently than our parents. Boomers and many Xers view technology as a means to an end; for us, technology is an end unto itself. It is a kind of "sixth sense" and extension of who we are, not just how we communicate.

Consider the smartphone. This one little device keeps us the most socially engaged and socially unengaged generation ever to exist. It can be an amazing tool for staying connected constantly with people we love while also serving as a barrier to unwanted social interaction. Nearly the same percentage of Millennials say the internet helps them make new friends (69 percent) or keep relationships they currently have (64 percent), as those who say it makes people more isolated (67 percent). Similarly, the same percentage believes technology makes everyone more efficient (69 percent) as those who say it results in people wasting time (68 percent).[20]

Technology has come to define us. We are the generation that grew up during the dot-com boom and bust. We were characterized by the widespread use of the internet during our early adolescence. Studies show technology has outweighed the terrorist attacks on September 11th as the most important "event" to shape our lives.[21]

Despite its imperfections, we believe there is very little that technology can't solve—from fixing diplomatic issues to curing diseases. If today's technology cannot solve the problem, we are assured that tomorrow's will. We have such confidence in technology because we have seen the incredible accomplishments it has already afforded us. Just think, the Jetsons cartoon was set to take place in the early 2000's. Although we may not have personalized robots that look like Rosie, we do have Siri on our iPhones and step trackers on our wrists.

MORE THAN FUN AND GAMES

Technology isn't just for keeping up with friends from college or sending around funny cat videos. Many of us are getting degrees online and taking formal and informal education courses via the web. Training and ongoing education is far simpler with growing access to webinars, educational "hangouts," and virtual project management. TED talks, Youtube channels, and Google Plus are all helping engage the Millennial motivation to constantly be learning something new.

Using social networking tools at work isn't just fun and games for us. If your Millennial employee has a quick question for a colleague at another firm, she may get on Facebook chat and send a message. Or she may use Twitter to look up recent news articles trending, or do background research on business networks through LinkedIn.

The thought of having a chat window on your desktop at work is offensive to many managers, but it is just the Millennial version of an open-door policy.

Technology is not just how we communicate. It is how we mobilize, how we socialize, and how we identify with each other and the world. The internet today has created a far flatter world for Millennials than for our parents and has helped give us a more global perspective.

THE LIES WE BELIEVE ABOUT TECHNOLOGY

Technology does pose a serious concern for Millennials. As youth-leadership author Tim Elmore explains, technology has hurt our generation in particular because we have content without context.[22] We can find the answers to essentially any question, but whether that answer is correct or relevant to our situation is not guaranteed. We have become so addicted to instant information and microwave-ready results that we have lost the discipline of research and reasoning.

We have bought the lie that technology allows us to endlessly multi-task. In a perfect world, we would live our lives uninterrupted without having to choose between mutually exclusive options. We want to listen to music while researching a biology paper while texting friends while downloading the last episode of whatever show while paying bills.

The ability to accomplish multiple tasks simultaneously is absolutely impossible. Science and common sense prove that the human brain has a finite ability to focus on multiple sensory inputs.[23] Every time the human brain is forced to flip from one task to the next, it is losing the momentum it developed from the last point of engagement. Millennials need guidance in this realm. We have become addicted to constant visual stimulation and have been conditioned to believe that constant change means productivity. Deadlines and checklists help us to focus our attention and drive toward successfully completing one project at a time.

Each generation enjoys more technology than the one before it (apart from maybe those who suffered through the Dark Ages). The younger generation will always have an advantage over older generation members who are typically less familiar with the latest technology. This is an opportunity in disguise. Rather than expending the cost for training existing employees in high-tech skills, managers can hire individuals who already have those skills—most of which have been acquired through cultural osmosis (which means that you don't have to pay for additional training).

For Millennials, technology offers a form of legitimacy. When was the last time you Googled a restaurant before eating there? Odds are the professionalism and accessibility of the website played a role in whether you spent your money there. In today's high-tech world, how an organization utilizes or fails to use the latest gizmos affects how Millennials view them. This is not to say you need to hire a "social media expert" for your company; in fact that title is so overused it has been rendered meaningless. However, it does mean that you need a Facebook page. And it's best to set up a LinkedIn and Twitter while you're at it.

Millennials also realize that technology saves money by consolidating multiple functions into one device. "Why would I pay for cable when I can stream any show I want directly on my laptop?" explained one Millennial to his awe-struck supervisor bragging about his 90-inch plasma. We don't need to buy four different devices to take photos, send emails, check voicemail, and make phone calls. It is all in one.

FACT 3: MILLENNIALS WANT TO BALANCE SCREEN-TIME WITH FACE-TIME.

Yes, we have been immersed in technology since infancy. However, we still crave real interaction with humans. In fact, I would argue *because* we have been so saturated with media, marketing, and messaging campaigns, we respond with the most authenticity to personal interaction away from a screen. In *Keeping the Millennials,* Drs. Sujanksy and Ferri-Reed explain, "They seem to almost intuitively understand the manipulative nature of marketing, and as a group, they seem to develop disdain for any advertising that is obviously too slick, too neatly packaged, or too good to be true."[24]

Millennials want to get personal. We are comfortable with initiating and maintaining relationships via technology (Hello—online dating), but if we are honest with ourselves, we want something more. Technology helps make communication easier, faster, and more interesting. But it will never replace the power of human interaction.

Larissa, a friend of mine, illustrates this principle. She had what appeared to be her dream job. Although she worked in an insurance office with typical hours, her schedule allowed her to come and go as she pleased and take meetings off-site. It also helped that Larissa's boss worked out of another location four hours away. Although they had a solid working relationship and communicated on projects and deadlines regularly, Larissa felt no emotional connection to her boss or the company. She would maybe see him or the other executives once a quarter, and usually it was in a conference room. When Larissa was in the office, she rarely interacted with her colleagues who were all 20 years her senior.

Despite liking her job and her boss, she found herself scrolling through hiring sites. Larissa just couldn't see herself working long term for what appeared to be a ghost. Soon enough, Larissa landed another job but was clueless about how to tell her boss (Did she email, call, drive down to meet him in person?). Two weeks later, Larissa still hadn't done anything (Millennials are also great at avoidance).

One morning, she got a call from her current employer congratulating her on her new position. Apparently Larissa's boss had met her new employer at a dinner party the night before and the former had shared how excited their firm was to bring Larissa on. Is it me or is it getting awkward in here? Although Larissa continued to move to her next job opportunity, she injured her relationship with her former employer and no doubt had her next boss wondering if she would continue avoiding confrontation with him.

Technology brings us together in an incredible way, allowing us to accomplish more in less time and often, at a lower cost. It can be a bridge or a crutch—depending on how it is used. Companies with high levels of technical communications (email, chat rooms, etc.) have a challenge when it comes to engaging employees in meaningful relationships away from the screen and helping them make human connections on the job.

WHEN TECHNOLOGY GOES TOO FAR

Technology can be a magical tool of communication, but it can also be a stumbling block for communicating effectively. For offices heavily reliant on email exchanges, we see a heightened sense of isolation and lack of trust in colleagues and managers. Directives may be taken out of context or completely misunderstood when read on a screen. It's like the childhood game of "telephone:" the message becomes more confusing with each degree it is removed from the source. If clear communication is a challenge, sending an email and then following up with a quick phone call or pit-stop at a coworker's desk will go a long way in clarifying intentions.

We are finding that employees who share their personal lives outside of work through social networking have more positive in-office relationships as well.[25]

Consider these tech-free networking ideas:

- Host an in-office happy hour.

- Have a guest speaker present during a "lunch and learn."

- Organize a volunteerism day across departments.

- Coordinate an off-campus lunch.

Look for opportunities to escape the digital world and encourage genuine and interactive employee engagement across generations.

"GENERATIONAL A.D.D"

As mentioned, most Millennials blur the lines between work life and home life. Don't be surprised if you engage in a conversation with your twenty-something employee and he jumps from what was on TV last night to the project deadline to his vacation plan next month.

What may seem like a generational disposition toward attention deficit disorder is actually an example of how we view our lives. We see our work during the day as equally relevant to our lives as what we do with family and friends. We don't like to compartmentalize our activities and so we use technology as a way to blend our worlds together. As we get older, we will learn more work-appropriate tactfulness, but we need your help to navigate these new waters.

Managers should help young employees learn what is and is not appropriate to share at the office. If you have an employee who doesn't seem to be self-correcting, have a manager or colleague set clear expectations on what the company culture stipulates when it comes to appropriately sharing personal information.

CHAPTER FOUR SUMMARY

Millennials love gadgets. From our phones to our computers to our music players—we love having the newest technology to play with. But technology is more than just a source of entertainment. Millennials use technology to constantly communicate with friends, family, and work associates.

It allows us to continue blurring the line between personal and professional worlds. We see no problem responding to emails while out to dinner with friends or texting our boss while we make our coffee in the morning. Similarly, Millennials take our personal lives to work with us and can get caught shooting a text to our significant others (or Mom) in the middle of a meeting. We love the flexibility that technology provides us to work from home, from the road, or on vacation.

We positively correlate technology with legitimacy, and see it as a way to improve communication, efficiency, and even save our companies money. We don't see why technology can't solve whatever challenge our generation may face. But despite our default reliance on technology, we crave personal and interactive relationships. What appears to be an addiction to a device is really an affinity for relationships.

TIPS FOR MANAGERS:

- *Keep their attention.*

When designing on-boarding programs, keep in mind Millennials communicate in short, visually stimulating, and succinct mediums. Diversify your technological outlets to engage Millennials in their various learning and communication styles. They respond well to hands-on and team-oriented training programs and want to see the practical application of the material they are learning.

- *Set house rules.*

Millennials do not see texting as an inappropriate form of communication. We do it in class, in church, and in meetings. Clarify when it is and is not appropriate. Develop a clear media policy and set standards across the board. If the VP is always on his phone but you nix Millennials' ability to text, you will not win points with young employees (and probably won't get them to keep the rules either).

- *Give them techie-training wheels.*

Allow for constructive uses of technology like social networking and email chains. Don't be afraid to let your Millennials install "chat" functions on their desktops but explain the intention is for work-related collaboration. Sending a quick message to a coworker may take less time and lead to more productivity than having to get on the phone, walk over to a desk, or even send an email. It's not there to make office gossip more convenient.

- *Save some green.*

Incorporate technology into virtual work and digital offices, cutting down on desk time and empowering your employees to do their best work in their best environment. Empower your employees to utilize available technology to accomplish company goals in an efficient and effective manner. Create a high-tech committee to test out how technology can save money, or host an in-office competition to brainstorm about how to update company practices with cutting-edge technology.

TIPS FOR MILLENNIALS:

- *Power down.*

Get out from behind the computer screen and ask clarifying questions of your supervisor in person. Be sensitive to the differing levels of comfort your older generation colleagues have with technology. Extra credit for offering to help them sync their email to their cell phones or set up their Wi-Fi router.

- *Take a poll.*

Ask your supervisor his or her preferred form of communication (email, phone, in person, text, etc.). Some managers may prefer email, and some Millennials may prefer texting. Understanding how your colleagues best give and receive news will improve overall communication goals of the organization.

- *Practice safe-texting.*

  Ask your manager or the human resources department about the social networking policy (being proactive shows that you will be mature with the responsibility they give you).

- *Clean up your act.*

  Sanitize your social networking sites. The internet is public property; many managers check your personal webpage when they are interviewing you, and may even monitor it after you are hired. Your social networking site is still a representation of who you are, and if you list your employer, you are self-identifying as an ambassador for your job as well.

BONUS: FREE SOCIAL MEDIA POLICY TEMPLATE

If you don't have a social media policy at your company, you need this resource. Clarify expectations and empower your young staff with skills to responsibly manage their social media life at work and avoid social media snafus.

www.socialmediapolicy.millennialsolution.com

CHAPTER 5
MYTH 5: MILLENNIALS ARE UNMOTIVATED

As a young account executive, Ben is assigned a client he is less than thrilled about. He knows that if he works hard and proves himself, he will be given more responsibility and hopefully a better batch of clients down the road. It is that hope that motivates him to put in late nights, file endless paperwork, and attend mundane meetings day after day. He is particularly disheartened on one of these days, when he spends hours putting together a community meeting that no one shows up to.

Soon after, Ben's boss brings him into his office. "I know this isn't the sexiest assignment and I bet it isn't what you thought you would be doing when you started with us," his boss, Phil, explains. "But what you are doing here is the bread and butter of our company. When you do good work for *your* client, it allows the rest of us to better serve our clients."

And then Phil says one simple thing that transcends any of his past interactions with Ben, clenching his young employee's loyalty to him forever: "Ben, I really appreciate all of your hard work."

His boss doesn't use charts and graphs to show the monetary benefit his work has, or even promise a promotion in the future. He simply shares how Ben's work makes him a valuable and appreciated member of the team. In less than five minutes he has helped his young employee understand that even the most mundane task has made a difference in the lives of everyone else in the company. Ben knows he isn't curing cancer, but he feels like he is able to make a positive impact in the lives of his coworkers and clients. That's good enough motivation for him.

I end with the myth that Millennials lack motivation because it is the most misused (and therefore underutilized) myth in the workplace. Unpack this fallacy and you will find yourself with a team of loyal and hardworking employees unlike any your company has seen before. The key to unlocking this potential involves understanding what Millennials really care about...and why.

WHAT LEADERS MILLENNIALS FOLLOW

Leadership plays a powerful role in motivating the Millennial. At its most basic level, leadership is simply the power to influence others. As a manager, you are a natural leader not only driving company profits, but also using your position to influence those in the company.

Two types of leadership are widely accepted in management training today: transactional and transformational.[26] Transactional leadership produces results as a result of or reaction to a request. Much like a financial transaction, there is an incentive to cooperate because the other party is gaining something of value on the other side of the deal, like a new title or a bonus. This may work, but it may not work for long.

The challenge with transactional leadership is that it is short-lived and temporary. A Millennial can put in ten hours of extra work a week for six months to get that raise his boss promised, but that doesn't necessarily mean he sees himself working that hard for him or her in another year.

Your management style may get a product at the end of the day, but it may come at the expense of an employee at the end of the year.

Transformational leadership inspires change from within. It empowers each individual to contribute his or her highest and best work. Yes, the follower will be motivated by the end result (like a raise or more responsibility), but is more likely to respond positively and consistently when he or she is inspired to do so. It also allows a boss to motivate employees over the long term, rather than baiting them with temporary rewards.

WHAT YOUR LEADERSHIP STYLE MEANS FOR MILLENNIALS

Let's see if you are a transformational or transactional leader:

- Do you change the roles and responsibilities of the position based on the personality and abilities of the individual who fills it?

- Do your employees demonstrate creativity spontaneously or only when they are compelled?

- Do your employees take on tasks independent of your direction?

- How often do you ask your employees how they are actually doing?

Transform your Millennial employees by getting to know them as individuals, engaging with them in non-traditional settings (outside of the office), and practicing the art of asking questions.

You may not believe it, but Millennials are human, and like most humans, they are inspired and motivated to action. But what incentivizes you and your colleagues to work harder and longer may be the very thing that pushes your Millennial workers away.

The first step to alleviating this tension is to open up the communication between yourself and your employees. Make incentives a personal conversation between two individuals, not an impersonal questionnaire or discussion about salary. When you sit down with your employees, you will learn from them firsthand what really inspires them to do their best work. Some questions you might ask include:

- Where do you see yourself in the next five years? Where will you be living and what will you be doing?

- How do you use your vacation days or time off?

- During which time of the workday are you most productive?

- Is having more responsibility and room to grow your experience a key motivator?

- What about this position originally drew you to apply?

By having an up-front conversation about what Millennials want to get out of the job, you will set expectations for yourself and for them. If these motivators change, encourage your employees to approach you and adjust their incentive structure accordingly.

FACT 1: MILLENNIALS WANT TO BE CHALLENGED.

Millennials are motivated to do well when they have high levels of expectations set for them. Studies have shown that where students were expected to perform well on coursework, their test results increased, in contrast to those who did not have high levels of expectation.[27]

Managers aren't doing their young employees any favors by setting sub-par expectations or using language that is condescending. It's far more helpful to challenge Millennials to assume responsibilities that teeter on the edge of their comfort zone (while being careful not to push them over!). This will show them you believe in their potential and aren't afraid of making small bets on their young success.

If they do produce sub-par results, take the time to assess the situation. What factors on their end hurt their success: was it user-error, a lack of experience, insufficient support, or bad information? Similarly, reflect on any external factors that contributed to the failure: did you provide incomplete facts, an unreasonable deadline, or a job outside of their skillset? Failing in the small things will help young employees be successful in the big things.

During my final year of college, I helped start a volunteer organization that brought youth together from across the city to become informed and activated to meet our community's needs. A local leader met me when the idea was still young and believed in the vision enough to help get it going. It wasn't a huge investment of time or resources, but he offered what time and advice he could. He even gave me a personal office to work out of and let the group use his facilities for our meetings free of charge. I will never forget one conversation I had with him and his wife after an event we had planned fell through. He said,

> I expect you to fall, Gabrielle. Not failing is a failure in itself. But when you do fall, know that we will be here to pick you up, dust you off, and let you keep running.

Knowing that I had the environment in which to learn, experiment, and grow helped me take my leadership abilities to the next level. I loved the challenge of working harder and doing better because I knew that even if the plan crashed and burned, I would still have the support system in place to keep going.

WHAT YOU DON'T KNOW ABOUT FEEDBACK

Feedback is essential. And I'm not just talking about an obligatory annual review, but the weekly—and sometimes daily—input that helps your employees know whether they are on the right track.

Millennials are accustomed to instant feedback. With the advent of social networking where we ejnoy instant responses to status updates, we are becoming conditioned to receiving instantaneous feedback on what we broadcasting. The shorter the time between action and feedback, the more likely it is that Millennials will associate the two events and be better prepared for future interaction.

When giving Millennials feedback:

- Give them context: Are you evaluating their overall performance, their role on a team, or their contribution on one project? Put a frame around the situation by explaining the four "W's": What, When, Where, and Why.

- Be specific: General praise can seem fake and general criticism can feel accusatory. Help Millennials understand exactly what they did that was praiseworthy or in need of improvement so that feedback becomes a tool for building a better work environment rather than a bludgeoning device.

- Keep it simple: The purpose of feedback is to help your employees, not confuse them. Focus on a simple instance they can use as a reference point for future   situations.

- Avoid assigning value: Before explaining what was *good, excellent, in need of improvement, etc.* let your employees explain their own level of satisfaction with their performance. This helps them take responsibility and see their performance from a manager's perspective.

- Above all, be honest.

Millennials don't want to just receive feedback; they want to give feedback as well. Allowing employees to review managers can seem threatening, particularly to employers who see performance reviews as a one-way street with lots of yield signs.

Even so, this caution does not negate the fact that Millennials see everything as a two-way conversation. Managers willing to let their Millennial employees give constructive feedback are pleasantly surprised to find Millennials expressing greater levels of respect and appreciation for leadership.

Much of this comes from the roundtable style of parenting we grew up with. Many Millennials were blessed with parents who included them in making family decisions on everything from vacation plans to remodeling the kitchen.

Letting those you manage have an opportunity to share how they work best under your management will help shed important light on your leadership style. If your company does not already employ a 360-degree review, it may be something worth pursuing through your human resources department. Whether via a formal process or an informal meeting over coffee, give your Millennial employees a chance to speak their minds.

FACT 2: MILLENNIALS WANT TO MAKE A DIFFERENCE.

Ask a Traditionalist what he does at work, and he might say, "Make a living." Ask a Boomer and she might say, "Make a profit." Ask a Xer and she might say, "Make a product." Ask a Millennial, and he will say, "Make a difference."

Millennials are very self-motivated, but they see incentives differently than the current structure most jobs offer. We are cause-driven, vision-focused, and passionate about change.

DEFINING SUCCESS FOR MILLENNIALS

Each generation has overlapping values, but each expresses and emphasizes them to different degrees. For example, each age cohort has its own definition of "success." For Boomers, accomplishment comes in the form of career promotion and monetary compensation. Boomers have worked long hours, spent their rising career years fighting for promotions, and delayed family vacations to get ahead. For Xers, success means having a healthy life/work balance that allows them to spend time with family and friends outside of their job. Many have come from divorced homes and now put a higher priority on spending time with their loved ones.

Success for Millennials looks like changing the world and leaving it a better, cleaner, and more just place for future generations. While Boomers and Xers strive for success, Millennials expect it.

Millennials may not be as concerned about climbing the corporate latter as their Boomer parents. However, position in the company is important. The ticket to motivating Millennials includes giving them more independence to create their ideal work environment, offering more significant responsibilities, or allowing for the opportunity to   manage   or   lead   others.

Millennials are building their own jungle gyms to exercise their excess talent. If we aren't getting the intellectual stimulation at work we need—or we don't feel fulfilled during our main job—we will start ventures on the side. The concept of the "side hustle" or "moonlighting" is one that is becoming widespread amongst a generation of young people desperate to share their talent with the world. The current job market and high cost of living has also forced many young people to work two, and sometimes even three jobs.

Millennials are twice as likely as Boomers to be serial entrepreneurs, owning and managing their own small business.

Don't let the Millennial love of challenge and innovation threaten their position in your company. Show us how our work today can help us thrive in our work tomorrow. Ask your 25-year-old office assistant with a passion for photography to take pictures at your next event. Invite your communications manager with a love of literature to start an office book club. By allowing your employees to be themselves and celebrate their uniqueness, you will help them flourish as individuals and feel appreciated and respected.

MILLENNIALS NEED MISSION

Millennials want to know that their company cares about people, not just profit. The book *Keeping the Millennials* explains, "Having been taught to value community service, this young generation has a preconceived sense of the type of social conscience they expect from any company they choose to work for."[28] It is for this reason, we see Millennials taking lesser paying jobs at firms with green energy policies and employee volunteer days. Millennials don't just expect companies to enact corporate responsibility to their employees; they believe in global responsibility to the planet.

Millennials aren't the only ones who are motivated by mission. It is an intrinsic human quality to want life and work to mean something. But Millennials are ambitious enough to walk away from a job if they feel it does not make enough of a difference.

If this question piques your curiosity, put together an anonymous survey of your office to find out what motivates your employees.

- How closely do you see your personal values reflected in the mission of the organization?

- How well does the organization execute its intended mission?

- Do you see your work directly contributing to the larger goals of the company?

- Do you struggle to see significance behind projects you are tasked with?

- How well does the organization retain qualified employees?

- If you were to leave the organization, which would you mostly attribute as the reason: pay, greater responsibility, challenge, or work environment?

- Would you recommend working at the organization to a close friend?

Asking these questions (as well as including opportunities for open-ended feedback) will help you have a better understanding of how employees within your organization find motivation on the job.

SHAPING COMPANY CULTURE

Remember that the culture of a company resides in its employees. They are the ambassadors of the organization to customers and the community. Empower them to experience the purpose for which the organization was created. No matter how mundane your "widget" may appear (from manufacturing carburetors to fixing copy machines), your company exists to make other people's lives better. Help employees connect their personal work to the saving work of your organization and their fulfillment on and off the job will skyrocket.

FACT 3: MILLENNIALS ARE MOTIVATED BY CHANGE.

Millennials have been raised in a fast-paced microwave culture, causing them to view change as healthy.

> They've adopted the pioneering American spirit and embraced it in the form of a profound belief in innovation—technological, social, and political. This belief is the hallmark of their generation. Millennials do not see a world of limits but one of possibilities in which anything can be accomplished with enough creativity and determination.[29]

We have been trained to move from one achievement to the next, one grade to the next, one project to the next, and one position to the next. Our upbringing has been linear in that the next step has always been mapped out for us—usually by either our parents, advisors, or career counselors. Many Millennials are getting thrown into the world of work and finding themselves asking, "What's next?" Managers can mitigate this tendency by creating an environment of change within the organization.

Diversifying our positions with complex tasks will also help excite and motivate us to bring our own Millennial creativity to the task at hand.

Allow your employees to "dream big" within the organization. Do they want to be the director over southwest sales, represent the company at a conference in Dubai, or travel and speak as a brand ambassador? Dreams are pivotal motivators and will help you and your employees connect on key points.

As author Jim Collins explains in *Good to Great*, managers need to focus on getting the right people on the bus, then work on what seat they sit in.[30] If you hire employees that fit the culture and mission of the organization, they will find their own way to contribute the most value. This is true at any age.

Many managers are hesitant to do this because it means their own positions may be threatened. No need to worry. If you are an effective manager, the only reason someone will be taking your job is because you will be moving on to a better one. When you pursue your own growth opportunities in your industry, you automatically open up new roles for those under your leadership.

YOUR PERSONAL EXIT STRATEGY

We don't often think about what the position we currently have in the company would be like if we moved on, but it is imperative to have a plan in place. Vacancies occur due to promotion, family challenges, dismissal, retirement, etc. Encourage fellow managers to begin grooming young employees to take positions of leadership with long-term prospects in the company. Remember to be vocal with your Millennial employees about the future you see for them. Don't leave it up to them to figure out that you see the potential for greatness in them. Remember, they enjoy constant feedback, especially when it is positive.

By starting early, you will be able to prime your top Millennial prospects for the future. If you tap into their motivators, your organization will find itself with a stronger pool of very well-qualified, highly competent, knowledgeable, and visionary leaders eager to advance its mission.

CHAPTER FIVE SUMMARY

By understanding what motivates your young employees, you will be able to create a win-win scenario in which both the organization and the employee mutually benefit. Find the motivator behind each of your employees and tap into what makes them the unique individuals they are. Whether Millennial or not, all people have something that uniquely inspires them.

Millennials are motivated by strong leadership. We are drawn to leaders that inspire us to be the best version of ourselves, who recognize where we are, and believe we have what it takes to be successful. Millennials commit themselves to transformational rather than transactional leaders and thrive when given feedback that is instant and situation-based. We want to know that our work is appreciated, our passions will be satisfied, and our itch to change the world scratched.

If we feel that all of our faculties are not being exercised at work, we will start our own business or side-projects. Our interests and abilities are like layers that can be unwrapped. Managers can help motivate Millennials by tapping into their distinctive motivators and creating opportunities for them to apply themselves and their passions on the job.

We love change and want to be challenged to do better or perform at higher levels. We are accustomed to being in a constant state of education and will feel invested in when we are provided continuing education opportunities to improve our contributive scope at work.

TIPS FOR MANAGERS

- *Make the grade.*

  Conduct a values assessment for employees as they transition or are hired. This will help them and you understand what they prioritize on the job and how to best motivate them.

- *Connect the dots.*

  Help your employees understand how the project they are working on connects to the overall vision of the organization. Include in memo lines a purpose statement section where they are asked how a project or position ties into the goal of the company; you can also turn it around on them and ask them to prove their worth!

- *Why did you hire them?*

  Reinforce who they are. Are they great with people, a whiz on computers, creative in their approach to communicating? By reminding them that you recognize their skills and see their unique contribution to the company, you will help Millennials keep their role in perspective of the organization. Look for opportunities to appropriately praise them for their contributions.

- *Reward results.*

  Provide incentive options such as days off, compensation, a new title, etc. By offering them options for how they will be rewarded, your employees will be more invested in achieving their goals. Plus, they will feel like their opinions matter.

- *Give back.*

  Find ways to give them positive feedback, especially when you are asking them to improve specific areas of their work.

- *A rose by any other name.*

  Give them input on their title. This will help them define what unique role they play in the organization while setting themselves up for a successful transition when they move to the next job.

TIPS FOR MILLENNIALS

- *Manage up.*

   Explain in your interview or onboarding process what motivates you. Do you enjoy the challenge of new opportunities? Love greater responsibility? Are you inspired by the mission of the organization? Help your future managers understand how to lead you.

- *Do your homework.*

   Research the mission of the organization and be prepared to articulate why it is in line with your personal views in interviews and discussions on promotions. Don't be afraid to remind them why they hired you.

- *Speak your mind.*

   If you see a disconnect between the values and daily practices of the organization, find an appropriate and respectful way to meet with your managing supervisor about it. This could be a great opportunity for you to demonstrate your ability to individually contribute to the greater good of the company, but proceed with tact.

BONUS: FREE CASE STUDY TO MOTIVATE
MILLENNIALS

We interviewed over 100 Millennials to discover why they would quit their job today. You may be surprised at the real reasons Millennials give for staying and will be empowered with skills to start motivating them today.

www.casestudy.millennialsolution.com

CHAPTER SIX
THE UNSPOKEN MYTH: MILLENNIALS HATE THEIR PARENTS

I couldn't believe we were arguing about this.

My mother and I were in a verbal wrestling match about who was right. I had called Mom for accounting advice soon after launching my training and consulting company, The Millennial Solution. Her thirty years of business experience included opening three restaurants and starting a successful roofing company with my father. I have asked her advice on nearly every other topic; getting her input on business seemed like a no-brainer.

The conversation began innocently enough. I was straightforward with my question: "What is the best way to keep track of your expenses?"

Tracking receipts was not a foreign concept for my mother. She is a business veteran, has an around-the-clock accountant, and has seen her fair share of audits. But I soon discovered her perspective was defined by experience—not necessarily relevance.

"Keep every one of your receipts and put them somewhere—like a file folder or shoebox—and give them to your accountant at the end of the year," she responded.

Seriously? I made zero effort to muffle my laugh. She must have been kidding. We share a sarcastic sense of humor, so it surprised me when upon further questioning, my mother assured me that she was serious.

"I'm sorry, Mom, but there is no way that I'm keeping receipts in a shoebox all year long. There's got to be a better way. Like an app or something."

That's what set her off. Despite her assurance, "That's just how things are done, Gab," I stood my ground...maybe a little too hard. I knew she was just giving me advice based on her experience, but I knew it was incredibly outdated, not to mention inefficient.

Soon after we both hung up, I realized how disrespectful I sounded in the conversation. I would call her back and apologize. But first, I opened up the App Store on my iPhone and searched "Track Receipts." As soon as I hit the search icon, my phone lit up with a colorful list of applications designed to track expenses, photograph receipts, and record mileage.

Jackpot.

I quickly downloaded the app with the best ratings and most extensive reviews. I decided to wait a few hours before calling Mom back to apologize.

When I did, she happily answered the phone as if nothing had happened. I explained that I wasn't frustrated with her; I was unsatisfied with her advice because I use technology to solve most of my problems. We had such different ways of problem solving. Her way seemed so archaic, but I realized that my desire to use technology came across as disrespectful. Her methods had worked for her with the knowledge and tools available at the time.

She readily accepted my apology. Before ending the call, I made sure to tell her this: "Hey Mom. You'll never guess the name of the app I downloaded…" I paused for dramatic effect and then shouted, "Shoeboxed!"

PARENTING THE MILLENNIAL GENERATION

Millennials take their own approach to the world. It only seems appropriate that the world would take a distinct approach to them.

Millennials were born during a time in history when parenting was done with intentionality, precision, and purpose. Books such as *Your Baby and Child: From Birth to Age Five* and *What To Expect When You're Expecting* flew off the shelves in the 1980s to provide direction and advice for knowledge-hungry parents of Millennials. What began as well intentioned—even sacrificial—parenting has turned into a hurdle that this generation must overcome.

Overparenting the Millennial generation was possible for many reasons. Many parents of Millennials rebelled against the hands-off approach their parents played in their own childhoods. Many vowed to make the lives of their children "better than their own."

However, the overworked corporate culture of the 1980s and '90s encouraged both parents to work longer hours and climb the corporate later. This led parents to spend less time with their children while retaining the ability to spend more discretionary income on their children. This meant more money for better, brighter toys and expensive college prep programs. The emergence of computerized technology also changed the game of parenting. It allowed television and video games to supplant busy overworked parents while also serving as a system of simple rewards or gifts for a generation of indulged children.

The overparenting culture in which Millennials were raised is the leading cause of Millennial entitlement. Millennials grow up with an expectation that things will be taken care of for them: from dinner to college applications.

Overparenting has also caused many adult Millennials to have difficult relationships with Baby Boomers. They expect Baby Boomers to take care of them as their parents did.

Nancy was my assistant while working for a non-profit organization near Washington, D.C. She was incredibly intelligent and well versed in economic theory and theology. I hired her specifically for her knowledge and ability to articulate the vision of our organization. She was self-directed when I needed her to be, but three months after hiring her, it became apparent that she lacked the ability to differentiate working peers from her parents.

While attending an economic conference in Seattle, Nancy slipped on a sidewalk curb and broke her foot. She called me soon after the fall and explained that the doctor had banned her from driving. She would need to work from home. I often worked from home, so I saw no real problem in letting her do the same.

After seven days, it became apparent that working from home was not working out for Nancy. She was slow in responding to email, did not follow my directions, and delivered projects days late. I'll give it to her. She recognized that her performance was suffering and asked if we could find a way to get her to the office.

It turns out that I passed by her place on my way into the office. I could swing by and pick her up. I didn't mind too much. It was only seven minutes out of the way and allowed me an opportunity to get to know her better. Besides, it got her out of the house and back to being productive.

The first week went well. I would text Nancy from around the corner so she was ready to go by the time I pulled up to her brick building. After about a week, she began to take longer to get ready, making me wait up to 20 minutes. One morning, after taking an additional 15 minutes to come downstairs, Nancy asked me to run an errand with her on our way into the office!

I tried to rationalize the situation. This was her first job out of college. She didn't understand protocol. She probably didn't realize that she was acting rude and entitled.

I started noticing how much time Nancy spent on the phone with her mom. I have an awesome relationship with my mom, so I didn't think anything of it. When our officemates started to comment, I took a closer look. Nancy's mom would call in the middle of the day, for seemingly no reason. You name the topic, they would talk about it: doctor's appointments, weekend schedules, finances, etc.

One week, Nancy was having a particularly hard time with her roommates; I counted six phone calls to her mother!

Managing Millennials, when you are one, can be tricky and awkward. However, I cared enough about Nancy's young career to give her a heads-up notice for future employers. Once a week, I took Nancy out to frozen yogurt to review projects, give feedback, and touch base. This was mutually beneficial; I love frozen yogurt and it offered a change of environment for our meetings.

That week, I decided to bring up the frequency of conversations between Nancy and her mom. At first, she was defensive - both verbally and physically. I was actually shocked at how quickly she shot back at me, "You talk to your mom too!" That wasn't the point, I explained. "It's starting to impact your behavior."

It was clear that Nancy saw me as more of a friend than a supervisor. But it was also clear that her mother had conditioned her to be dependent on her for decision-making. It was as if Nancy had no muscles to think critically about her life.

As a consultant working with companies to retain Millennial talent, I now see the much larger impact caused by this style of parenting. There are millions of Nancys in the workforce who are highly intelligent and very skilled, and yet are having a difficult time adjusting to adulthood. It eventually became apparent that Nancy was not a good fit for our firm. She left two months later, but taught me an invaluable lesson on the importance of growing up.

GETTING YOUR MILLENNIAL KIDS OFF THEIR PHONES

Sitting in a cute coffee shop in the heart of Brooklyn, two young twenty-somethings sat across from one another. It was clear they had been there a while. Their heads were down and their phones were out. They were texting.

After about 15 minutes of watching these girls silently type away on their phones, I turned and asked a question. "Hey, sorry if this sounds weird. But I've been sitting here and haven't seen you say anything to each other. Who are you texting?"

Apparently I hit a nerve. The girl sitting closest to me half smirked and half smile as she answered, "Each other."

As we discussed in the "Addicted To Technology" chapter, Millennials use technology to communicate constantly. This necessity to stay connected can be a great tool for communication. It can also be the biggest detriment to being understood.

Millennials may not consider or even see the absurdity in the situation that I just described. They may consider it completely normal to hold text conversations while in public. Their parents and managers think differently.

When interacting with a Millennial who is prone to gluing a thumb to her smart device, separate the Millennial's behavior from her personality. It is tempting to ban technology completely from them, especially the worst offenders, but just because someone is acting in a rude way does not make him or her a rude person. More often than not, the perpetrator is not aware of how his actions are being interpreted. Give examples of how his actions appear. Explain clearly that when his attention is absorbed by technology, it creates more difficulty in relating to and interacting with him. It is important to emphasize that the reason you get upset with Millenials' use of technology is that it gets in the way of you having a relationship with them.

Parents of teenagers used to ask questions such as, "Should I let my teenager have a computer in their room?" and "When should I let my teenager have a phone?" Parents today are pressed to find answers to those questions and even more. They are asking these questions:

- "How much time should they spend on their phones?"

- "Is it okay to take their phones away as punishment?"

- "How do I protect them from online predators?"

- "How can we have a conversation when they're attached to their device?"

Technology has not only changed how the world works; it has also changed family dynamics. For parents, communicating with their kids is dependent upon their willingness to adapt to their communication style.

Some parents refuse to give in. Phil is one of these parents. I met Phil while speaking in Southern California. He became upset when I explained the real reason why Millennials text instead of calling on the phone. Phil pulled me aside after the talk and argued that not requiring his children to communicate on his terms was disrespectful. As a successful business owner, I knew that Phil understood the fundamentals of business communications.

I asked Phil if he ever changed how he communicated to reach different types of clients. His response was abrupt. "Of course." I followed up with another question. "Did you change the medium of communication or just the language?" He responded again. "Both. Of course." I explained that, just as he was willing to change the way he talked to a client, we should all be ready to adjust our communication style so that the other person hears and understands what we are saying.

Parents are leaders. As a leader, you have the sole responsibility of reaching your Millennial child. It may be awkward—even difficult—to begin using social media or texting to communicate to your kids. However, the benefit of growing your relationship far exceeds the cost of comfort that you may be currently experiencing.

TURNING MILLENNIALS INTO ADULTS

I stood in front of a room full of defense contractor managers. I had been brought in to explain how to keep Millennials from quitting. Halfway through my 90-minute presentation at their annual meeting, a hand shot up in the back.

A woman quickly introduced herself and explained that she was "busy managing three needy Millennials" (her words, not mine). Her honesty was refreshing and yet stark. At the end of her question, which turned into a statement about what's really wrong with Millennials, she asked, "Can't I just tell them, 'Because I said so?'"

It took everything in me to not look as shocked as I felt. She was clearly serious, and yet it was shocking for me to believe that any manager would treat her adult staff like young children.

I successfully restrained the urge to freak out and responded with a question. "Thanks for your perspective. Do you have any Millennial children?" It turned out that she had two sons in their twenties. "Great. Do you talk to them like this?" She blushed as she explained that she didn't, at least not anymore.

Eric Berne is a renowned psychotherapist who authored the theory of transactional analysis. According to Berne, there are three ego states: *Parent, Adult* and *Child*. In a Parent ego state, you are telling others what to do. In an Adult ego state, you are collaborating as equals. In a Child ego state, you are allowing others to make decisions for you. As I shared this theory in my response, I explained that if she addressed her Millennial employees in the Adult Ego state, they would have the option of acting like a child, but they will most likely respond in their Adult ego state.

Transforming Millennial children into Millennial adults is a process. Many parents I have worked with don't know when and how to let go.

Not sure how to do it? Start here.

Set expectations. Whether you are taking them off your phone bill or asking them to find their own place, communicate clearly to your Millennial kids at least two months before a major shift will begin. They will be able to plan accordingly, and it also gives you an opportunity to think through options with them.

Be consistent. If you are asking them to find their own place, don't reject their request for help. Do not, however, take this as a sign that you should do the work for them. Consider yourself a highly paid consultant – take on the projects you want, but don't do the actual execution of the work for your "client." Your child may come to you for strategic advice and wisdom, but they should not be coming to you for the execution. Saying one thing and doing another is a major parental faux pas.

Let them fail. It's hard, especially at the beginning. But your Millennial child will fail - hopefully a lot. How you celebrate their failure will determine how they view their capacity to rise above the situation. Sara Blakely, CEO and Founder of Spanx, explained in a *Business Insider* interview how every evening, her father would ask the kids in her family what they had failed at. He was more excited about them failing than excelling![31] Create opportunities that celebrate their failure and challenge them to keep going.

Be tough. Do you remember when they finally stopped sucking their thumbs? If your kids were anything like me growing up, breaking habits didn't come easy. I can still remember my dad sitting me down and explaining why sucking my thumb wasn't what "big girls" did. Although I was a child, he talked to me as an adult and used reason to help me understand why I needed to let go of my childish habit. Your adult children may not be sucking their thumbs—at least we hope not. Maybe they're texting at work or wearing sweatshirts to formal events. Rather than scolding them, empower them with the knowledge and context for why their behavior isn't appropriate.

WORKING WITH YOUR MILLENNIAL CHILDREN

Running a family business sounds great. However, talk to anyone who has done it and you will quickly realize its vast level of difficulty.

Mixing blood and business involves heightened emotions. You are at a higher risk of offending someone or taking business decisions personally. Despite the hazards, there are millions of successful businesses owned and operated by kin.

I was speaking at a business conference in Baltimore, MD, when a young woman raised her hand in the middle of my session. I love it when the audience interacts, so I jumped at the opportunity to answer her question. This young woman introduced herself and explained that she worked for her father, who is a lawyer.

Every week, her dad asked her to file depositions. The process used in the office included printing the depositions, putting them into an envelope, stamping them, and taking them to the local post office. After about two weeks of following office protocol, this young woman had had enough. There had to be an app for this!

After some Googling, she discovered a secure app that allowed her to accomplish the same task at half the time and expense. The next week, when her father asked her to file the depositions, she decided to ask a question: "Why?"

Her father immediately became defensive at his daughter's defiance. He shot back, "As your employer, I am telling you what to do." She pushed back. "Yeah, but why that way?" That really got to him. "As your father, I am telling you this is what you need to do." You can imagine how well that went over.

The young woman explained to the group that it had never occurred to her—until my session—that her question had seemed disrespectful. She asked why because she wanted to show her father a better way of doing something. She wanted to be involved in the decision-making process, rather than being told what to do all the time. She wanted to have freedom to do her job.

After speaking on stages around the world, I have collected similar responses from twenty-somethings in the workforce. Many admit that they don't realize when their action are interpreted as entitled or their questions come across as needy.

Working with many companies owned and operated by multi-generational families, I can tell you that this story is not unique. Whether you are working with your Millennial kids, volunteering with them, or asking them to work around the house, there are seven fundamental keys to keep in mind.

1. Let them make mistakes, and don't emotionally punish them afterward.

We all mess up when we are first starting out. Rather than letting them fail on the big things, give them small projects to muck up first. Managing your kids can be tough. However, it is imperative to keep your actions in the workplace from affecting your interactions outside of the office. Conditional love brought on by business can fester and kill what's most important: your relationship.

2. Be there to answer questions, not to solve their problems.

Parents step in to help out their children. Many continue this practice well into their adult lives. This affects their level of self-sufficiency on the job. I see this even in companies that aren't operated by the same family. Many Millennials have had other adults make major decisions on their behalf and therefore expect any authority figure to come to their aid.

3. Keep your relationship focused on achieving a goal.

Teams in every industry—from sports to medicine—include individuals from different backgrounds, experiences, and perspectives who come together to achieve a shared goal. When you focus more on the product and less on your feelings about it, you will be able to preserve your relationship with your Millennial kids.

4. Remember humility. It may be hard to admit that you don't know, but Millennials will respect you more for it.

Transparency with your kids can be especially difficult. Parents think, "If they see my weaknesses, they won't respect me." With Millennials, the opposite could not be truer. Millennials love it when leaders show vulnerability because it assures us that their leaders are relatable, authentic, and trustworthy.

5. Involve them in making decisions.

In the heat of battle, it seems more expedient to make decisions on behalf of the company without involving your

Millennial staff. However, every decision brought before you is an opportunity for you to teach Millennials about the way you think. One day, they will be leading the company, and would really benefit from understanding your thought process, approach, and assessment structure.

6. *Don't treat them any better, or any worse, than other employees.*

Parent-bosses have an extra level of accountability placed on them by their employees. They cannot show too much favoritism toward their kids, but they can't punish them either. Employees are quick to call "favorites" when the boss's kid gets a promotion or a raise. However, this reality should not encourage harder treatment for your kids either. The key is to be transparent in all of your delegation and hiring procedures so as to secure the respect of your entire team.

7. *Say, "I trust you."*

These three words put together are the most powerful management tool that any leader can possess. Millennials want to be taken seriously and given responsibility to fail or succeed.

A PARENT'S GUIDE TO GIVING FEEDBACK

Life isn't perfect. Relationships are difficult to maintain. Awkward and difficult conversations only complicate things.

As a parent, you have a duty to help your children make wise life decisions. However, I have found that the difficulty is to *not* give advice. For most parents, it's harder to determine when to stop than to start.

The first and most fundamental rule in giving Millennials feedback is to ask for permission. Susan was the mother of a very opinionated 21-year-old son. When he decided to drop out of college because he couldn't decide on a major, she became concerned. Concerned is an understatement. Susan became inconsolable. She would call her son multiple times a day to tell him why he needed to go back to school. She would send friends to his apartment to talk him out of dropping out. She even staged an intervention with his father and cornered him with questions about his plans to make money.

Susan's actions severely damaged her relationship with her son. She was motivated by love and a deep desire to see him succeed. However, she was providing hostile and unsolicited advice to a young man who needed direction, wisdom, and clarity.

The second rule of feedback is to wait for your Millennial to ask for advice. Millennials actually want to know what their parents think. They may not ask for your approval formally, but they will eventually come to you with an opportunity to provide feedback.

The third rule of feedback is to ask for ways they would want you to give them feedback. We do this constantly in our corporate relationships. We take personality tests at work to determine how those around us think, work, and communicate. However, we rarely reflect on how those in our family prefer to share their thoughts and feelings. Have a conversation about feedback with your Millennial at a time when they are not asking for advice and you are not giving advice. Ask how they prefer to receive feedback and have them provide an example of feedback that was well received, and feedback that they did not receive well.

After all, what good is advice that gets ignored?

ADVICE FROM MOM

To get a parent's perspective on how parents can interact with their kids on major life decisions, I turned to my mother, also a bestselling author and speaker, for advice. This is what she shared.

1. *"Support their idea, and don't make it about you."*

It's too easy to give self-serving advice. For instance, your child is thinking about applying to colleges and you don't think twice before suggesting your alma mater. Find opportunities to come alongside their dreams rather than inserting your ideas, insights, and opinions.

2. *"Don't squelch their ideas; suggest another thing they could try."*

Let's say your Millennial has an idea that is either foolish or dangerous. Rather than criticize their idea, brainstorm with them to discover a more appropriate alternative. Your 16-year-old daughter may think it's a great idea to backpack through Europe during Spring Break. Don't attack her ambition. Recognize the core desire and work with her to find something suitable and mutually agreeable.

3. *"Give practical advice."*

Sometimes Millennials want you to just listen. Other times, they are desperate for direction. Avoid saying things like, "Well, what I would do," or, "This is what I did when I was your age." Direct them to a resource, give perspective on what others have done, and provide multiple options for them to think through.

4. *"Help them through and give confirmation along the way."*

As we have addressed in the "Entitlement" chapter, Millennials have an expectation for constant feedback.

They are accustomed to extrinsic praise—trophies, hugs, and verbal responses. They are not as motivated by intrinsic affirmation—such as beating their personal best. Confirmation does not mean unsolicited or undue praise. It does mean affirming the small, positive changes they are making along the way.

5. *"Ask clarifying questions." Millennials are young.*

They don't have all of the answers and are bringing an idea to you for two reasons: affirmation or advice. Sometimes it's difficult to decipher which scenario you are facing. By asking clarifying questions, you can help them gain a better grasp on their idea or proposal. Before launching into your list of queries, it is always a good idea to ask them for permission. Try, "I love your passion. I really want to get a good understanding of what you're talking about. Is it okay if I ask a few questions to help me understand?"

6. *Help them see themselves in the future."*

As their parent, you have a completely unique perspective on your children. You see them like no one else sees them; you love them like no one else can love them. This means you know their natural talents, personal passions, and intellectual aptitude. You are perfectly positioned to coach them into their destiny. As a senior in high school, going to the prom seems like the most important thing in the world. In your twenties, finding an awesome job becomes more important than single events. Priorities change as your perspective widens. Help your Millennial kids gain perspective on the situation at hand by projecting who they are and what they are doing in the future. When minor disagreements or drama would come up, my mother would remind me, "Will you be talking about this in three or four years? Of course not. So why let yourself get distracted?"

7. *Don't take it personally when they don't take your advice."*

The best thing and worst thing about advice is that it's free. You can have the most profound wisdom, and yet there will always be someone who ignores it. When your Millennials don't heed your advice, avoid taking it personally. They are on their own path of discovery. Nagging them until they see things like you will never work—however tempting it may be. Respect them as individuals rather than forcing them to agree with you.

My mother and I have had an incredible relationship growing up, but as she readily admits, she had a hard time determining when and where to give feedback. The words of wisdom she shared are the result of countless conversations where we both agreed to be teachable.

I had to learn how to empathize with my mother when she was giving advice. I had to practice seeing things how she saw them, rather than resting in my own shallow perspective, while she had to be willing to relate to me while respecting my privacy and discretion.

We are all in process. Parenting the Millennials is the most challenging and rewarding job imaginable. We are a generation that is bursting with potential and craving direction. Parents have the responsibility and opportunity to partner with their Millennial children, helping them to discover who they were created to be. After all, we're not created to do this alone.

CHAPTER SIX SUMMARY

While Millennials are different from their parents, that doesn't mean they necessarily intend disrespect by questioning their parents' process of getting things done, or by finding more technology-friendly solutions. Turning Millennials into adults (who don't act either in a rude or entitled way) can be as simple and as complicated as setting expectations, letting them fail, and involving them in decision-making processes. It can be especially difficult to forge a relationship as a parent-boss to a Millennial, since this involves the additional layer of other employees' perceptions. Remember that this difficult task is also greatly rewarding; Millennials really do want your advice and feedback as they work out their own independent path.

ADVICE FOR PARENTS

- *Be patient.*
  We are all in process and the more patience you are with your Millennial kids, the more you model maturity. It is natural to get frustrated, but don't let your frustration or disappointment become known by your Millennial child.

- *Ask for permission before giving advice.*
  No one like unsolicited advice—especially when it comes from a parent. By asking first, you are demonstrating a permission-based approach to leadership. It also shows your Millennial that you respect their time and privacy.

- *Treat your Millennial adult children as adults first, as your children second.*
  Knowing when to "cut the chord" can be difficult. Clarify the situation by having open conversations with your kids to adjust your parenting to fit the season of life they are in. Ask things like, "Am I doing a good job letting you be an adult?"

ADVICE FOR MILLENNIALS

- *Learn to be empathetic.*

  Your parents aren't perfect. The older you get, the more you will discover just how human they are. Rather than get frustrated with them for not understanding, ask questions to discover what their point of view is. Even if you don't agree, you will learn from the situation and gain a broader perspective.

- *Start with respect.*

  To get respect you must first respect others. Check with your parents to make sure your actions are conveying respect. You may think texting them back when they call, or wearing jeans to church is appropriate; however, these small actions may come across as disrespectful. Show respect to those older than you, and you will increase your influence, network and proximity to top leadership.

- *Provide feedback for your parents.*

Help your parents out by providing feedback that is specific and respectful. Help them understand how you prefer to communicate, what times of day you prefer to catch up and how you expect them to treat your friends or significant other. Major miscommunications always stem from a lack of communication.

CHAPTER SEVEN
CONCLUSION

I couldn't see where the little voice was coming from but there was one guess as to whom it belonged. It had seemed that the world's most inquisitive six-year-old sat behind me on the six-hour flight to California. "Where are we going?" "Can I stand up in here?" "What was that sound?" "Who is driving the plane?" There didn't seem to be a question this little guy didn't have.

When he initially arrived at his seat, the little boy was excited and slightly scared as to what the experience was going to be like. He wanted to know the ins and the outs of air travel, the history of flight, why everyone else seemed so calm, and why he had to stay seated but the flight attendants didn't. His mother patiently answered each of his questions. We continued to ascend and his queries became less frequent. Before long, he became more comfortable with his new surroundings and focused away from the *how* and *why* of flying, to the *what*—in this instance, the experience of being on an airplane.

FINDING THE "WHY"

As humans, we are naturally programmed to want to know *why* something exists. The entire academic field of science exists for the sole purpose of asking and answering these questions. Getting to this core question of *why* allows us to mine key motivators from human action.

This book has been written to help answer many of the questions managers have about Millennials and clarify the misconceptions about this upcoming generation.

THE FIVE MYTHS RECAPPED

There are five myths that have been holding leaders of all levels back from really utilizing the full potential of the Millennial generation.

Like most stereotypes, those assigned to the Millennial generation are somewhat accurate. However, they don't need to stand in the way of your organization's productivity. By identifying the myths and properly adjusting for them, you can transform your young employees from liabilities to be managed into assets waiting to be leveraged.

1. Millennials aren't entitled; they are ambitious.

We are a generation of recent graduates eager to put our degrees to work. When others ask, "Why?" Millennials will ask, "Why not?" We see challenges as opportunities and have been empowered with high expectations set for us by our parents and mentors. We have been told from our childhoods that we can and will change the world.

If Millennials see a need in an organization, they will take the initiative to fill it. Although recognition is an important motivator, Millennials will generally volunteer to take on opportunities simply because they see something that needs to be done. We want to give back and would prefer to be a part of a group when we do so.

We walk into organized associations and expect the customs and culture to adjust according to our preferences. We have been conditioned as children, students, and now young adults to believe we can change how the world works if we set our minds to it. We are looking to use our collective powers for good, but we need to be managed in a way that harnesses our ambition and does not crush our fantastical passion.

2. Millennials aren't disloyal; they want to be mentored.

Millennials are relationship skeptics. We don't care what you know, unless we know that you care. We long for mentoring and investment from company leaders and managers. We don't commit to organizations as much as we associate ourselves with individuals.

A job is an extension of our identity and a representation of who we are. We want to know that what we do makes a difference and will search for mission alignment with our employer. We want to be engaged in a real way and are terrified we will wake up in five years sitting at our keyboard, doing the same job we are doing now. We get bored easily, but that is only because we have so many interests; we would like to commit ourselves and our talents to those who appreciate all that we have to offer. We are looking not only for people to give us a paycheck, but for individuals who will coach us and lead us to our destiny.

3. Millennials aren't independent; they are team players.

Millennials want to be a part of something bigger than themselves. We want to help others succeed and gain a sense of fulfillment when we work toward a shared goal. We have been conditioned to operate as a team and feel most comfortable when we are able to share responsibilities with others—no matter their ages.

Teamwork means we can give as much or as little as we want, but it also means that we can share our victories with our friends and colleagues. We are used to building things with our parents and have had shared responsibilities in family decision-making from our childhood. We consider ourselves not only our parents' children, but their friends, colleagues, and legacy projects.

Millennials crave diversity in multiple forms including age, experience, expertise, gender, and ethnicity. Placing us on teams that celebrate our own unique contributions while letting us learn from others will help us become acquainted with the mission and vision of the organization.

4. *Millennials aren't addicted to technology; they want to be engaged.*

Millennials have been marketed to our entire lives and know what surface-level relationships look and feel like. We long for real (and consistent) interaction. We use technology to stay constantly connected and feed our need for community. We gain validation from our collective experience and use email, text messaging, and social media to be updated in real time on what others are doing.

It is the Millennial default to turn to technology to research and resolve issues. We believe that technology makes things faster, better, and cheaper. In the old days, collaboration took place in a board room; now it is happening on interactive digital platforms like chat rooms, video conferencing, and newsfeeds.

5. *Millennials aren't unmotivated; they need to be empowered.*

Millennials want to be recognized because of who they uniquely are, not what they uniquely do. It is important for us to know that we can work toward a goal, but we want to know first and foremost that we are appreciated for who we are apart from how we get our organizations ahead.

Think of your Millennials as battery-operated devices. Plugging us in to our power source (or unique motivator) will give us the boost of inspiration and direction we need to keep going. We don't expect the job to be easy. In fact, if it is too simple we will get bored and move on! We want to be challenged to grow and empowered to achieve the goal. We want to make a difference in the world—even if our impact only reaches one person.

You have the chance to mine generational gold.

The Gold Rush in the mid-20th century turned rowdy entrepreneurs and determined adventurists into millionaires overnight. Ambitious men from all of the country rode west in hopes of striking gold and creating a better life for themselves.

To the naked eye, there was no way to determine where gold hid beneath the surface of the California countryside. Some dredged mountains in search of treasure, leaving behind gaping holes and scars still visible today. Others mined in the foothills, extracting gold from the inside of mountains. Still others spent long hours hunched over a pan in ice-cold streams pulling out flecks that shimmered.

Finding gold takes consistent and determined effort— whether it is discovering gold in yourself or in your company. Each of us has within us the potential for greatness. Great leaders, great parents, and great managers can identify and optimize the hidden treasure they see in those they influence.

Each of us will spend nearly one-third of our lives at work. By investing just a little more time understanding who the members of this next generation are (and who they are not), you will improve the quality of time spent with Millennials at work, at home, and beyond.

TAKING THE NEXT STEPS

This handbook is meant to be a guide for managers, parents, and leaders on generational engagement with Millennials. More work needs to be done in this field and new research is on managing Millennials in the workplace is being debuted daily. Some of it is anecdotal, some of it is empirical, but few research faculties are relevant to what a manager is experiencing now.

This book is meant to consolidate the quality research that has been conducted and forge it as a tool to help you and your company manage and motivate your Millennial talent. This guide, and the accompanying resources at www.millennialsolution.com, have the practical steps and relevant tips to help you see how this information can start working for you.

It is one thing to know *about* Millennials. It is another thing to actually *know* Millennials themselves—what makes them unique, what inspires them and what gets them to work harder and with more enthusiasm. By introducing yourself to Millennials and understanding we are more than our reputation, you will find yourself engaging with a more spirited, diverse, and—dare I say it?... humble group of young people than you ever expected.

Millennials have been given the title, "The Next Greatest Generation." Whether it sticks or not, the reality is that this next generation of entrepreneurs, politicians, teachers, and coaches has the drive and determination to make a difference. We are now looking for those who have gone before us to lead and empower us as we prepare to take on leadership positions of our own.

The next generation is here. We are the Millennials and we are here to work, here to make a difference, and here to stay. Will you lead us?

NOTES

---

[1] U.S. Department of Commerce, Census Bureau, Current Population Survey (CPS), "Annual Social and Economic Supplement," 2012.

[2] Doug Lederman. (May 17, 2013). "Enrollment Decline Picks Up Speed." *Inside Higher Ed*.

Retrieved from
http://www.insidehighered.com/news/2013/05/17/data-show-increasing-pace-college-enrollment-declines

[3] Strauss, William & Neil Howe. (1992). *Generations: The History of America's Future, 1584 to 2069* (p. 421). Fort Mill, SC: Quill-House Publishing.

[4] "What Gen-Y Thinks about Pay TV and Cable Cutting." Ideas and Solutions. Retrieved from
http://www.ideasolutions.com/cable-cord-cutting-study-information.html.

[5] Alder, Harry. (1994). "NLP the new art and science of getting what you want." London, UK: PIATKUS Publishing.

[6] Hershatter, A. & Epstein, M. (March 5, 2010). Millennials and the world of work: an organization and management perspective. *Journal of Business and Psychology*, Retrieved from
http://www.springerlink.com/content/84q74131rt766284/fulltext.pdf.

[7] Supplemental Research Brief from National Business Ethics Survey. (2010 June 8). Millennials, gen x and baby boomers: who's working at your company and what do they think about ethics? Ethics Resource Center. Retrieved from http://www.ethics.org/files/u5/Gen-Diff.pdf.

[8] Thurman, Susan. (2013). "NSHSS Scholar 2013 Millennial Career Survey Results. The Emerging Workforce: Generational Trend." National Society of High School Scholars. Retrieved from http://www.nshss.org/media/1583/nshss-career-survey-2013.pdf.

[9] Goudreau, Jenna. (March 7, 2013). "7 Surprising Ways to Motivate Millennial Workers." *Forbes Magazine*. Retrieved from http://www.forbes.com/sites/jennagoudreau/2013/03/07/7-surprising-ways-to-motivate-millennial-workers/.

[10] Marston, Cam. (2007). *Motivating the "What's in it for me?" workforce: Manage across the generational divide and increase profits*. Hoboken, NJ: Wiley. Retrieved from http://www.ncbi.nlm.nih.gov/pmc/articles/PMC2868990/#CR64.

[11] Putnam, Robert. (August 7, 2001). *Bowling Alone: The collapse and revival of the American community*(pg. 58). New York, NY: Touchstone Books by Simon & Schuster.

[12] *"New Report Illuminates America's "Silent" Dropout Epidemic."* (May 2, 2006). Civic Enterprises Research commissioned by the Bill & Melinda Gates Foundation. Retrieved from http://foundationcenter.org/pnd/news/story.jhtml?id=133800007.

[13] (Gen WE p. 14).

[14] Lancaster, Lynne C. and David Stillman. (April 6, 2010). *The M-Factor: How the Millennial Generation Is Rocking the Workplace* (p. 231). New York, NY: Harper Business.

[15] Sujansky, Joanne and Jan Ferri-Reed. (2009). *Keeping The Millennials: Why Companies Are Losing Billions in Turnover to This Generation- and What to Do About It* (p.153). New York, NY: Harper Business.

[16]Fry, Richard. (August 1, 2013). A Rising Share of Young Adults Live in Their Parents' Home Pew Research Center. Retrieved from http://www.pewsocialtrends.org/2013/08/01/a-rising-share-of-young-adults-live-in-their-parents-home/.

[18] Lancaster, Lynne C. and David Stillman. (April 6, 2010). *The M-Factor: How the Millennial Generation Is Rocking the Workplace* (Robert Half Survey, p. 243). New York, NY: Harper Business.

[19] Millennials: Confident. Connected. Open to Change. (February 2010). Pew Research Center. Retrieved from http://pewresearch.org/pubs/1501/millennials-new-survey-generational-personality-upbeat-open-new-ideas-technology-bound.

[20] Greenberg, Eric H. and Karl Weber. (2008). *Generation We: How Millennial Youth are Taking Over America And Changing Our World Forever*. New Zealand: Pachatusan.

[21] Greenberg, Eric H. and Karl Weber. (2008). *Generation We: How Millennial Youth are Taking Over America And Changing Our World Forever* (p. 24). New Zealand: Pachatusan.

[22] To learn more about Tim Elmore and his Growing Leaders Blog visit http://growingleaders.com/blog/category/generation-iy/.

[23] Hamilton, Doug. (October 2, 2008). "Think You're Multitasking? Think Again." National Public Radio special. Retrieved from http://www.npr.org/templates/story/story.php?storyId=9525 6794.

[24] Sujansky, Joanne and Jan Ferri-Reed. (2009). *Keeping The Millennials: Why Companies Are Losing Billions in Turnover to This Generation- and What to Do About It* (p.189). New York, NY: Harper Business.

[25] "Public Relations, Social Media and Job Satisfaction." Special presentation from Simon Fraser University. Retrieved from http://www.sfu.ca/grow/sera/pr/.

[26] Ingram, David. Transformational Leadership Vs. Transactional Leadership Definition. Small Business Chronicle. Retrieved from http://smallbusiness.chron.com/transformational-leadership-vs-transactional-leadership-definition-13834.html.

[27] Elikai, Fara and Peter W. Schuhmann (2010). An Examination of the Impact of Grading Policies on Students'

Achievement. Issues in Accounting Education, 25(4), 677-693.

[28] Sujansky, Joanne and Jan Ferri-Reed. (2009). *Keeping The Millennials: Why Companies Are Losing Billions in Turnover to This Generation- and What to Do About It* (p.137). New York, NY: Harper Business.

[29] Greenberg, Eric H. and Karl Weber. (2008). *Generation We: How Millennial Youth are Taking Over America And Changing Our World Forever* (p. 29). New Zealand: Pachatusan.

[30] Collins, Jim. (October 16, 2001). *Good to Great: Why some companies make the leap… and other don't. New York, NY:* Harper Business.

[31] http://www.businessinsider.com/sara-blakely-spanx-ceo-offers-advice-redefine-failure-retail-2016-7

Made in the USA
San Bernardino, CA
12 February 2018